Marilyn MONROE

Cover to Cover

SECOND EDITION

Published by

krause publications
An F&W Publications Company

700 East State Street • Iola, WI 54990-0001
715-445-2214 • 888-457-2873
www.krause.com

Please call or write for our free catalog of publications. Our toll-free number to place an order or obtain a free catalog is (800) 258-0929.

Library of Congress Catalog Number: 99-60080
ISBN: 0-87349-596-9

Photography by Skip Drew.

Every attempt has been made to identify and credit sources of cover photos. The publisher would appreciate being informed of any discrepancies in this or subsequent editions.

Table of Contents

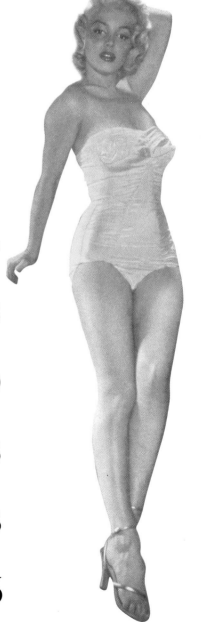

Dedication

I want to dedicate this book to a dear friend I recently lost. Gerald Arena had a heart of gold. He was a dedicated Marilyn Monroe fan and collector, and he was truly genuine in his friendships with fellow human beings. Gerald has set an example that those who knew him shall always strive to live by.

We will miss him dearly.
Gerald Arena (1959-2002)

Acknowledgments

Such a book as this would not be possible without the help of a number of people.

I owe a debt of gratitude to my friend, Tina Garland, who graciously allowed me to photograph many Marilyn magazine covers from her personal collection. Thanks as well to my friend Bartoli for supplying several covers from her collection. In this same regard, I must thank my longtime Marilyn collector friends from Italy, Giovanbattista Brambilla and Angelo Urbinati, for supplying color slides of rare Marilyn covers from their collections.

Thanks must go to my friend and fellow Marilyn Monroe author, George Zeno, who kindly assisted me with identifying when and where particular photos of Marilyn were taken. This was very useful in arranging the covers chronologically, based on Marilyn's age when the photo was taken.

I wish to thank the legendary Mamie van Doren for the fantastic job she did writing the foreword. She is one of the kindest individuals that I have ever been acquainted with.

I would also like to thank the various estates that represent selected Marilyn Monroe photographers for working with me regarding the use of copyrighted photos. These include: The Archives of Milton H. Greene (Joshua Greene), the estate of Andre de Dienes (Shirley de Dienes), and the estate of Bruno Bernard (Susan Bernard).

Thanks to my wife, Linda, and my two sons, Robby and Nathan, for putting up with me once again, while I feverishly compiled another book on my favorite blonde.

Much gratitude is owed to my friend Skip Drew of Milton, Wisconsin, who once again did a superb job of photographing the magazine covers.

Thanks as well to my agent, Claudia Menza, for her excellent representation.

Last, but certainly not least, I'd like to express my gratitude to my publisher Krause Publications, as well as Paul Kennedy and Maria Turner, the editors who made the publication of this book possible.

Foreword

Marilyn is an enduring mystery. These days, she has become all mystery and icon, and less human.

It is a measure of Marilyn's growing icon status that more and more people claim to have known her so well. People who may have driven past her house now claim to have been her close friends.

Those of us who really did know her, however, still remember the flesh-and-blood Marilyn as a presence who is at times in conflict with the icon.

I remember Marilyn as a giggle in the darkness as she watched in secret during my early screen test at 20th Century-Fox. She still knew me as Joanie, a brash kid who used to sneak into the Ambassador Hotel's pool to swim. I had known her as Norma Jeane, a girl, slightly older, who was already doing modeling photo shoots by the pool. But she was Marilyn, and she watched the screen test with the kind of good humor not always seen among rivals, then or now.

I remember her also in jeans and sweatshirt coming to and from the house of her acting coach, Natasha Lytess, as I was coming to or from my lesson.

I remember Marilyn as the one who opened the door for women in Tinseltown. Without her, perhaps none of the rest of us could have seen the way that would lead to what is now "Hollywood Glamour." And the trials she endured on the journey would not deter the rest of us, though they might cost a life.

Marilyn would frolic with even the president because actresses in general need too much love. (Although recent revelations about JFK's health would seem to indicate that their affair might have been a bit less torrid than we would like to believe.) Audiences sometimes imagine excitingly different lives for us, and certainly, we encourage those fantasies, but I have never met an actress—a real glamour-girl-type sexy actress—who didn't have a deep, dark lonely streak inside.

And I remember Marilyn at the Russian Tea Room in New York, sad about the end of her JFK affair and troubled by what appeared to be the end of her career. At the time, neither she nor I knew what the rest of the story would be, not seeing in the vodka on the rocks where time would take her memory.

In the end, nothing can detract from Marilyn's essential qualities of vulnerability and beauty. And none can deny that she is a shining light from out of the past that *means* Hollywood Glamour. Clark Kidder's second edition of *Marilyn Monroe: Cover to Cover* once again focuses that light ever so sweetly.

Photograph by Julie Strain, September 2002.

Mamie Van Doren is the sole survivor of the women known as the "Three M's"—Marilyn, Mamie, and Mansfield—three of the most recognizable sex symbols ever to grace the silver screen. Born Joan Lucille Olander in Rowena, South Dakota, she signed her first contract with Universal Studios in 1953 and rose to stardom as the "bad girl" in some of Hollywood's most memorable teen-age cult films. Van Doren co-starred with such greats as Clark Gable, Tony Curtis, Mickey Rooney, and Donald O'Conner and has appeared on such shows as Red Skelton, Jack Benny, Merv Griffin, Steve Allen, Hard Copy, Entertainment Tonight, Larry King Live, and Good Morning America. On February 1, 1995, she received her star on the Hollywood Walk of Fame. She currently lives in Newport Beach, California, and graciously agreed to update her foreword from the previous edition of this book.

Introduction

As a teen-ager, I would sit and listen to my grandfather, Earl Kidder, reminisce about Marilyn Monroe. He would often ask himself the question, "Why in the world would such a beautiful girl, who had everything, take her own life?" Although it's doubtful that anyone will ever know the exact answer to that question, my grandfather had inadvertently sparked an interest in this mysterious blonde within me. I picked up a copy of Norman Mailer's biography on her, and after reading it, became even more intrigued.

My interest continued to grow as the years passed, and I soon began hunting auctions and rummage sales in search of Marilyn memorabilia. Some of my first finds were her cover appearances on *LIFE* and *Look* magazines. It was in a contemporary issue of *LIFE* that an article about a huge Marilyn Monroe collector appeared. A resident of New York, George Zeno was shown standing on a ladder in front of his wall of Monroe magazine covers. It was at this point that I became aware of the vast number of covers Marilyn had appeared on, not only in the United States, but around the world. The hunt was on!

This book features a culmination of the nearly 18 years I have spent diligently seeking out Marilyn's magazine cover appearances from all corners of the world. I have arranged the covers in chronological order, showing the metamorphosis, if you will, of Norma Jeane into Marilyn Monroe. They will take you from her earliest days to the final cover appearances during her lifetime, as the magazines of the world said their final goodbye. Ironically, it would not be the end of Marilyn Monroe's cover appearances, as she continues to appear on the covers of magazines worldwide to this very day.

The covers that follow will begin with the brunette Norma Jeane, a budding new model recently discovered at a parachute plant, and will progress to show the new starlet who would eventually have her hair straightened, and later lightened to a shimmering blonde. The covers will take you through a succession of movie costumes Marilyn donned in her various films, studio publicity photos, and striking candids, as she climbed from just an extra to one of the biggest stars that Hollywood had ever seen, and ultimately, one of the greatest icons of the Twentieth Century.

Where the photographer of the cover is known, he or she is listed, along with the title, date of the publication, and its country of origin. I have also provided a value range for all publications. These values should be considered a guide, as prices fluctuate depending on numerous factors. The prices given are generally for magazines in very good to near-mint condition.

The photo on the facing page depicts Marilyn Monroe and the editor of *Look* magazine in 1953. They are admiring Marilyn's cover appearance, which also featured Betty Grable and Lauren Bacall from *How to Marry a Millionaire*.

The Life of a Legend

Marilyn Monroe was born Norma Jeane Mortenson on June 1, 1926, in Los Angeles, California. She was the illegitimate child of Gladys Baker. Though her father's last name was listed as Mortenson on her birth certificate, her real father was presumed to be C. Stanley Gifford. Marilyn's mother was a film cutter for the Hollywood Studios, but due to mental illness, Baker was committed to an institution.

Norma Jeane was placed in a succession of approximately 12 foster homes, as well as an orphanage. By 16, Norma Jeane was facing another move, when she met and married a neighbor boy, James Dougherty. Jim was a merchant marine, and while he was overseas, Norma Jeane went to work at a parachute plant to help the war effort. It was at this plant that army photographer David Conover pulled Norma Jeane to the side to take some photos for an army magazine to help boost the morale of the troops. He commented to Norma Jeane on how photogenic she was and encouraged her to pursue modeling. Little did he know that she would do just that!

Norma Jeane signed on with the Blue Book Modeling Agency, which was operated by Emmeline Snively, and was soon hired by various glamour photographers, her image being used in magazine ads and on covers. Norma Jeane soon took a screen test at Fox and was hired for some bit parts in a couple films, only to be let go after her contract had expired. In the meantime, she was persuaded to change her name to Marilyn Monroe.

Marilyn's big break came in 1950 with what would be a very pivotal role in her career. At the persuasion of Johnny Hyde, her agent and lover at the time, Marilyn was cast in *The Asphalt Jungle*, starring Louis Calhern. For the first time, audiences really noticed her.

A succession of films followed, until 1952, when a reporter discovered that it was indeed Marilyn Monroe who graced the top of a certain nude calendar. Marilyn explained to reporters that she was hungry—and out of work—when she agreed to pose for the nude photographs. Fortunately, the public was sympathetic and lined up in droves to see her next film. *LIFE* magazine put her on its cover and printed a full-color photo of the famous calendar pose in the accompanying article.

The stage was set. Marilyn was just a heartbeat away from reaching superstar status.

Marilyn had the starring role in several films released between 1953 and the time of her death in 1962.

While filming *River of No Return* in 1953, Marilyn began to date baseball legend Joe DiMaggio. Before too long, the couple was married and flew off to Japan for their honeymoon. While there, Marilyn was asked to perform in several shows for the troops in Korea. She accepted. Braving the bitter cold, clad only in skimpy gowns, Marilyn came down with pneumonia. However, the show went on, and Marilyn later called the whole experience "the highlight of my life."

While filming the famous dress-blowing scene for *The Seven Year Itch* in 1954, tensions began to grow between Marilyn and Joe. It seems that even two pairs of underwear failed to conceal what they were meant to, and each time Marilyn's dress would blow up in a gust of wind to reveal all that was private in Joe's mind, his face got redder and redder. Not long after, Marilyn and Joe were divorced.

Marilyn, determined to get better roles and not be typecast as a "dumb blonde," went to the famed Actor's Studio in New York City. She studied under Lee Strasburg. It was during her stay in New York that she decided to form her own production company with friend and photographer, Milton H. Greene. It would be called appropriately, Marilyn Monroe Productions. Marilyn gained critical director approval for any future films. She was the first star to challenge the studios—and win!

With her new confidence and power, Marilyn glowed in her next films: *Bus Stop*, *The Prince and The Showgirl*, and *Some Like It Hot*.

In 1956, a romance began between Marilyn and the famous playwright Arthur Miller. They soon married. Dubbed the "hourglass" and "the egghead," the couple struggled on through diversity, including a couple of miscarriages. Finally, it was all too much, and the marriage ended in divorce soon after Marilyn completed filming *The Misfits*, which Arthur had written for her. Ironically, it would be her last marriage—and her last film.

In 1962, filming began on *Something's Got To Give*. Marilyn missed countless days of filming due to a terrible sinus infection. This cost the studio a great deal of money, as it held up production. It was during this time that Marilyn was asked to fly to Washington and sing "Happy Birthday" to President Kennedy. This infuriated the studio, and it decided to fire Marilyn. A few months went by and the studio had a change in heart, and rehired Marilyn, even increasing her salary.

Before Marilyn could begin refilming, she was found dead in her Brentwood home on the morning of August 5, 1962. She had died of an overdose of barbiturates, perhaps by accident. To this day, her death is surrounded by controversy, and there are countless theories of what really happened that fateful night in 1962.

Regardless of what happened, the world lost a very special human being... a lost little girl who strived her whole life for a fulfillment that she would never come to realize.

Time Line

June 1, 1926—Norma Jeane Mortenson (a.k.a. Baker) is born to Gladys Baker in Los Angeles, California.

June 27, 1941—Norma Jeane Baker graduates from Emerson Junior High School in West Los Angeles, California.

1942—Norma Jeane enrolls in University High School, West Los Angeles, California.

June 19, 1942—Norma Jeane marries her neighbor's son, James Dougherty.

June 26, 1945—David Conover photographs Norma Jeane at parachute plant.

August 2, 1945—Norma Jeane enrolls at the Blue Book Modeling Agency, run by Emmeline Snively.

April 26, 1946—Norma Jeane's first U.S. appearance on the cover of a national magazine, *Family Circle*.

August 26, 1946—Twentieth Century-Fox signs Marilyn to a standard player contract.

September 13, 1946—Norma Jeane divorces James Dougherty.

1947—Marilyn gets her first bit part in the film *Dangerous Years*.

August 25, 1947—Fox drops its option on Marilyn.

March 9, 1948—Marilyn signs a contract with Columbia Studios.

September 8, 1948—Marilyn is dropped by Columbia Studios.

1948—Marilyn appears in *Scudda Hoo! Scudda Hay!* and *Ladies of the Chorus*.

August 15, 1949—Marilyn begins filming *A Ticket To Tomahawk*.

1949—Marilyn appears in *Love Happy* with Groucho Marx.

January 5, 1950—Marilyn begins filming *The Fireball*.

1950—Marilyn films *The Asphalt Jungle*, obtains a pivotal role opposite Bette Davis in *All About Eve*, and also appears in *The Fireball* and *Right Cross*.

December 10, 1950—Fox signs Marilyn to another six-month contract.

1951—Marilyn appears in *Hometown Story*, *As Young As You Feel*, and *Let's Make It Legal*.

April 18, 1951—Marilyn begins filming *Love Nest*.

May 11, 1951—Fox signs Marilyn to a seven-year contract.

March 13, 1952—A reporter reveals that it is indeed Marilyn on a popular nude calendar.

April 7, 1952—*LIFE* magazine puts Marilyn on its cover and reproduces the nude calendar inside.

1952—Marilyn appears in *Clash By Night*, *We're Not Married*, *Don't Bother To Knock*, *Monkey Business*, and *O. Henry's Full House*.

September 2, 1952—Marilyn is grand marshal of the Miss America Parade in Atlantic City, New Jersey.

November 1952—Marilyn begins filming *Gentlemen Prefer Blondes*.

1953—Marilyn stars in *Niagara* and *How To Marry A Millionaire*.

December 1953—Marilyn appears on the cover of Playboy, becoming the magazine's first centerfold.

January 14, 1954—Marilyn marries Joe DiMaggio in San Francisco.

February 1954—Marilyn performs in several shows for the troops while on her honeymoon in Korea.

11

Summer 1954—Marilyn stars in *River of No Return* and *There's No Business Like Show Business*.

August 10, 1954—Marilyn begins shooting *The Seven Year Itch*.

September 15, 1954—Marilyn films the famous skirt-blowing scene in front of the Trans-Lux Theatre in New York City.

October 27, 1954—Marilyn is granted a divorce from Joe DiMaggio.

December 31, 1955—Marilyn signs her final contract with Fox, guaranteeing her $100,000 per film.

May 3, 1956—Marilyn begins filming *Bus Stop*.

May 14, 1956—Marilyn appears on the cover of *Time* magazine.

June 29 and July 1, 1956—Marilyn marries playwright Arthur Miller in first a civil ceremony and then a Jewish ceremony.

November 17, 1956—Marilyn completes filming of *The Prince and The Showgirl* in England.

November 6, 1958—Marilyn completes filming *Some Like It Hot*.

November 4, 1960—Marilyn finishes filming *The Misfits*, her last completed film.

January 20, 1961—Marilyn and Arthur Miller divorce.

April 23, 1962—Marilyn begins filming *Something's Got To Give*.

May 19, 1962—Marilyn sings "Happy Birthday" to President John F. Kennedy at Madison Square Garden in New York.

June 1, 1962—Marilyn celebrates her final birthday, her 36th.

June 8, 1962—Fox fires Marilyn for tardiness during the filming of *Something's Got To Give*.

July 12, 1962—Marilyn meets with studio bosses to resolve differences, and succeeds. Filming was to begin again by the end of the year.

August 5, 1962—Marilyn's housekeeper, Eunice Murray, finds her dead at her home in Brentwood, California.

Cover to Cover Price Guide

Marilyn Monroe easily could be called the original cover girl. Her very appearance on a magazine cover ensured a considerable increase in issue sales. Of course, this was true only after she had attained superstar status around 1952. Before then, she had graced the covers of many U.S. and foreign magazines as simply just another pretty face.

Marilyn began her career as a model in 1945 when she was just 19. She learned early on how to best use makeup and would later be a photographer's dream. She took great pride in applying most of her own makeup.

By 1946, Marilyn began to appear on numerous covers not only in the United States, but in other countries as well, often unidentified. Her early U.S. cover appearances tended to be on romance or men's types of publications. Some of the more risqué photographs had to have clothing painted on in order to comply with censorship laws. Marilyn was really ahead of her time and continuously taunted the censors.

Marilyn's magazine cover appearances are some of the most popular Monroe collectibles, with some fetching prices in the hundreds of dollars. These appearances number more than 1,000 to date, and she continues to grace covers in nearly every country in the world, more than 40 years after her death.

In general, magazines with collectible Monroe covers come in four sizes: pocket (4 x 6), digest (5½ x 7½), standard (8½ x 11), and large (10½ x 14). In most cases, size makes little difference when determining the value of the magazines. The covers most sought-after by collectors are those in which Marilyn occupies the entire cover.

Descriptions of Magazine Grades

The estimated values for each magazine are listed from the very good to near-mint range. Here is a guide to help with determining the proper grade for a particular collectible:

Mint
Never used. Just as it came from the printer, regardless of its age. Appears to be new.

Near-Mint
Looks perfect at a glance. Only minor imperfections evident in the form of tiny tears, corner creases, or spine stresses.

Very Fine
An excellent copy. Minimal surface wear is evident. Staples may show discoloring through paper. Spine may show stress lines.

Fine
An above-average issue with minor but noticeable cover wear. Some discoloring at staples. Minor wear at staples and spine, but not serious. Corner creases evident. Multiple creasing will drop it a grade. Cover may be slightly loose.

Very Good
General wear evident. Staples may be rusty. A store stamp or name may be written on cover. Pages may be a bit brittle. A small amount of chipping may be evident or a small piece of a corner may be off. Cover may be stained, spine split, cover creased and slightly soiled. Minor tape repair may be noted.

Good
Below-average copy. Numerous creases; light soiling and staining. Cover may be detached and have both small and large tears. Spine may be split. Pages may be yellowed and a little brittle and may display various areas of chipping.

Fair
Complete issue but with a few pages missing, writing on cover, chunks missing. Cover may be detached and have tape repairs. A good reading copy. Pages brittle and also yellowed with age.

Poor
Much of the cover may be missing, as well as several pages. Heavily soiled with brittle pages. Good reading or research copy. Good copy to clip ads from.

Leader Magazine. April 13, 1946. England. Andre de Dienes. This is Marilyn's first solo cover. It is ironic that it was not even on a U.S. magazine. The photo was taken in 1945.

....$500-$700

14

Zondagsvriend. September 27, 1951. Holland. Andre de Dienes. This cover photo was taken in 1945. When recalling her early days in foster homes, Marilyn once remarked: "I don't think any of the people I lived with ever were knowingly unkind to me. It's just that there was never any love or affection for me. They never hugged or kissed me. They'd…just pat me on the head, like a puppy. And they kissed their own children."

....$200-$300

Pour Tous Films. August 27, 1946. France. Andre de Dienes. Marilyn is shown here frolicking on a sunny California beach in 1945. Leon Shamroy, who gave Marilyn a screen test in 1946, once recalled the event: "I got a cold chill. This girl had something I hadn't seen since silent pictures. She had a kind of fantastic beauty like Gloria Swanson, when a movie star had to look beautiful, and she got sex on a piece of film like Jean Harlow."

....$50-$90

de Prins reporter. August 14-28, 1948. Holland. Andre de Dienes. This 1945 photo of Marilyn was retouched by censors. They carefully painted fabric over Marilyn's exposed belly. It was taboo at the time to even show a belly button. My, have things changed!

....$200-$350

15

Art Photography. March 1952. United States. Andre de Dienes. This photo of Marilyn was taken on Mount Hood in Oregon in 1945. Even at 13, Marilyn was named "Oomph Girl" of Emerson Junior High in Los Angeles.
....$75-$125

Sir!. December 1952. United States. Bruno Bernard. This cover photo was taken in 1946. Marilyn once remarked: "In Hollywood, a girl's virtue is much less important than her hairdo. You're judged by how you look, not by what you are. Hollywood's a place where they'll pay you a thousand dollars for a kiss and fifty cents for your soul. I know, because I turned down the first offer often enough and held out for the fifty cents."
....$75-$125

Intimita. August 1, 1947. Italy. Unknown. This cover photo was taken in 1946. Marilyn once said: "I like to be really dressed up or really undressed. I don't bother with anything in between."
....$200-$400

Intimita. August 6, 1948. Italy. Unknown. This cover features a photo of Marilyn taken in 1946. Photos from this session with Marilyn were used to promote her 1948 film, *Scudda-Hoo, Scudda-Hay*. Marilyn had a bit part in the film, which was her first.
....$200-$400

PROVEN COLD CURE Dr. LINUS PAULING'S NEW BOOK!

A PLAN TO CUT YOUR CAR REPAIR BILLS BY 30%

PAGEANT

MARCH 50¢

ENJOYING THE MALE BODY— A Woman's Guide From Head To Toe

Memories of Marilyn Monroe

A LOVER REMEMBERS HER PLUS FLESH & FANTASY PHOTOS YOU'VE NEVER SEEN

Pageant. March 1971. United States. Andre de Dienes. This cover features a photo of Marilyn taken in 1946. Marilyn once proclaimed: "I want to be an actress. I want to be an artist. I am qualified, and I want to prove it." ....$80-$100

Allas veckotidning. October 15, 1954. Sweden. Andre de Dienes. This dreamy cover photo, taken in 1946, is sad in retrospect. We can only hope that Marilyn is resting as peacefully now as she appears here. This early photo brings to mind what was one of Marilyn's favorite songs, Judy Garland's "Over the Rainbow." ....$150-$225

Allas *tidning* 35 ÖRE Nº 41 15 okt.

Nya Klädpriser! –Läs om Gary Cooper

Hela Varlden. July 1948. Sweden. Laszlo Willinger. This photo of Marilyn was taken in 1947. It was also used on the cover of the September 1947 issue of *True Experiences* in the United States. The photographer, Laszlo Willinger, was originally from Hungary and became famous photographing many of Hollywood's biggest stars, beginning in the 1930s.

....$400-$600

19

Noir Et Blanc. July 20, 1953. France. Unknown. The photo on the right was taken circa 1948. The photo on the left was taken in April 1953 at the premiere of *Call Me Madame*. Marilyn once said: "I was never used to being happy, so that wasn't something I ever took for granted. You see, I was brought up differently from the average American child because the average child is brought up expecting to be happy."
....$50-$75

Cuéntame. December 5, 1951. Argentina. John Miehle. This photo of Marilyn dates to 1948, and also graced the cover of a 1951 issue of *True Romance* in the United States. When *Ladies of the Chorus* was released in 1948, Marilyn commented: "I kept driving past the theater with my name on the marquee. Was I excited. I wished they were using 'Norma Jeane' so that all the kids at the home and schools who never noticed me could see it."
....$100-$150

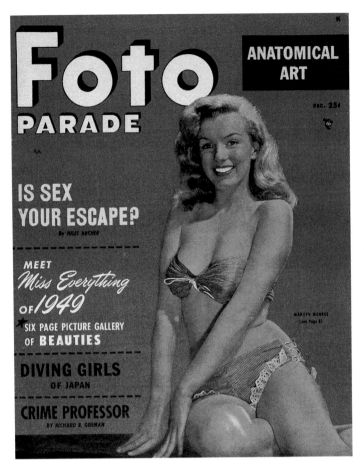

Foto Parade. December 1949. United States. Laszlo Willinger. Paul Parry, one of the earliest photographers of Norma Jeane/Marilyn, once had this to say about his first meeting with her: "I was sitting in my office chinning with a couple of other fellows one day when this girl—her name was Norma Jeane Dougherty then—came in and asked if I thought she could be a model. I'll never forget it, because she was wearing a pink sweater, and the other two fellows just fell right off their chairs. Could she!"
....$150-$200

Scope. November 1952. United States. Laszlo Willinger. This photo was taken in 1949. Marilyn once explained to a reporter how she used to be called "Norma Jeane the Human Bean" and how things changed when she began to "mature." She said: "When I walked into the classroom, the boys suddenly began screaming and groaning and throwing themselves on the floor. For the first time in my life, people paid attention to me. For the first time, I had friends. I prayed that they wouldn't go away."
....$90-$150

Regal. June 1953. France. Laszlo Willinger.
This cover photo was taken in 1949.
Marilyn once commented:
"I think if other girls know how bad
I was when I started, they'll be encouraged.
I finally made up my mind I wanted to be
an actress, and I was not going to let
my lack of confidence ruin my chances."
....$80-$100

Regal. May 1953. France. Laszlo Willinger.
This cover photo was taken in 1949. Marilyn once
remarked: "I think cheesecake helps call attention to you.
Then you can follow through and prove yourself."
....$80-$100

Chicago Sunday Tribune. August 6, 1950. United States. Unknown. This cover features an unusual photo taken in 1949 of a red-haired Marilyn. It was in late-1948 that Marilyn's hairline was "squared off" by doctors, eliminating the rounded "sweetheart" shape that it previously had.

....$200-$300

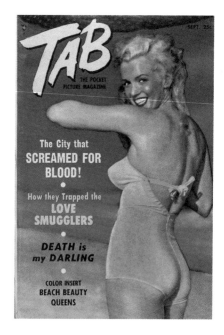

Noir Et Blanc. February 25, 1953. France. Possibly Weegee (Arthur Fellig). This cover photo was taken at the Jones Beach pool in 1949, while Marilyn was in New York on a tour to promote *Love Happy*. Marilyn once commented: "When you're a failure in Hollywood, that's like starving to death outside a banquet hall, with smells of filet mignon driving you crazy."
....$45-$75

Tab. September 1953. United States. Andre de Dienes. This photo was taken at Jones Beach, on the north shore of Long Island, New York, in 1949, while Marilyn was on a cross-country tour to promote her film *Love Happy*, which starred the Marx Brothers. Marilyn once described the scene: "My arms are up to embrace an imaginary partner, but note my hair was a shade lightened because it always went dark in black and white."
....$60-$80

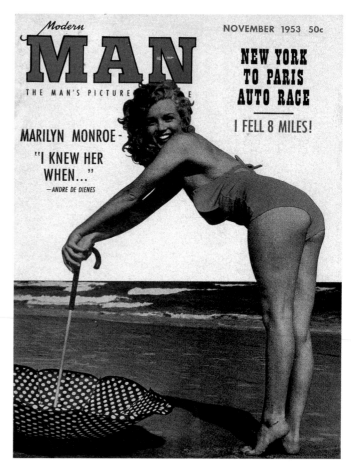

Modern Man. November 1953. United States. Andre de Dienes. This cover photo was taken in 1949. Marilyn once made this comment about sex: "Look, I'm a woman. Sex is part of nature, and I'm part of nature. I don't understand all the whispers about the subject. I don't do anything that's wrong—I just behave as a female. What's wrong with that?"
....$40-$80

Noir Et Blanc. July 16, 1952. France. Andre de Dienes. Marilyn frolics on Jones Beach on Long Island in 1949. Actor Jack Paar once had this to say about Marilyn, with whom he co-starred in *Love Nest*:
"I fear that beneath the facade of Marilyn, there was only a frightened waitress in a diner."
....$85-$125

Serena. May 6, 1954. Italy. Unknown. An unusual 1950 photo of Marilyn is featured on the cover of this Italian magazine. It appears to be a candid shot. Marilyn once said, "I've tried almost everything—at least once."
....$50-$90

Sissi. August 17, 1959. Spain. Unknown.
This cover features a photo of Marilyn that was likely taken in late-1949. The upper left photo was taken in 1950 and shows Marilyn with her then-lover, Johnny Hyde. Hyde was still married when he proposed to Marilyn, but Marilyn declined. Hyde's days were numbered, due to a bad heart condition. He was worth a great deal of money. If Marilyn were the gold digger she was made out to be, she would have married him to gain access to his fortune. Hyde was instrumental in Marilyn's career and helped land her important roles. He died before she attained superstardom.
....$40-$50

Uge-Revyen. January 15, 1952. Denmark. Unknown.
This photo of Marilyn was taken in late-1950 to help promote Marilyn's role in *The Asphalt Jungle*. Marilyn received the following letter from some student fans after seeing the film: "A bunch of us fellows went down to see *The Asphalt Jungle*, and when you came on the screen, we almost lost our eyeballs. We didn't even know who you were."
....$50-$100

BILLED BLADET

MARILYN MONROE — *For 2 Aar siden ukendt — I Dag Publikums Yndling* Nr. 1 SE SIDE 20–21

Nr. 45   4. November   15. Aargang   1952   60 Øre

Billed Bladet. November 4, 1952. Sweden. Bill Burnside. This publicity photo of Marilyn was taken in 1950. Marilyn once said: "My first contract with 20th Century-Fox was like my first vaccination. It didn't take."

....$90-$130

Garbo. October 3,1953. Spain. Bill Burnside. This cover features a publicity photo of Marilyn taken in 1950. Marilyn once said, "I think that work and love are the only things that matter."
....$40-$70

Novell Magasinet. Circa 1951. Sweden. John Engstead. This cover features an inset of a 1950 photo of Marilyn used to promote her role in *All About Eve*.
....$30-$50

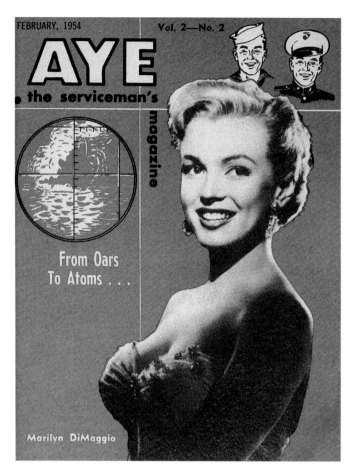

Cover to Cover

Aye. February 1954. United States. John Engstead. This servicemen's magazine features a 1950 publicity still of Marilyn for her film *All About Eve*. Too bad for the serviceman who had nice teeth as Marilyn once said: "A man with perfect teeth always alienated me. I don't know what it is, but it has something to do with the kind of men I have known who had perfect teeth. They weren't so perfect elsewhere."
....$50-$100

Hela Varlden. 1951. Sweden. John Engstead. This publicity photo of Marilyn was taken in 1950 to promote *All About Eve*. In 1951, Marilyn made this comment to reporters: "Someday I want to have a house of my own with trees and grass and hedges all around, but never trim them at all— just let them grow any old way they want."
....$100-$175

29

The Pittsburgh Press
ROTO
Magazine
Sunday, July 1, 1951

Marilyn Monroe . . . GIs' Favorite Pin-Up   See Pages 8 and 9

Roto Magazine. July 1, 1951. United States. Ed Clark. This cover features a publicity photo of Marilyn taken in 1950. Another photo from this session was used on the cover of *Movieland* magazine in 1953. Of relationships, Marilyn said: "I never fooled anyone. I've let men sometimes fool themselves."

....$150-$225

Novela Film. January 1, 1955. Yugoslavia. Unknown. This publicity photo of Marilyn was taken in 1950 and was used to promote her role in *All About Eve*. The woman who stole many hearts once said, "Husbands are chiefly good as lovers when they are betraying their wives." ....$40-$80

Radio Revue. May 22-28, 1955. Germany. Unknown. This is a 1950 publicity photo for *All About Eve*. Actress Natalie Wood once said of Marilyn: "When you look at Marilyn on the screen, you don't want anything bad to happen to her. You really care that she should be all right…happy." ....$50-$90

Screen-Radio-Television. November 19, 1950.
United States. Unknown. This unique photo of Marilyn
was taken in 1950. The caption on the cover reads:
"Pretty Pilgrim – only a meanie would give Marilyn
Monroe the bird – even on Thanksgiving. She has a thin
part in *All About Eve*."
....$500-$700

Home and Life Magazine. December 2, 1950.
United States. Unknown. This cheesecake photo of
Marilyn was taken in 1950. Even though she appeared to
have no problem showing skin in front of a camera,
Marilyn wasn't quite so confident in herself, having said,
"I always felt I was a nobody, and the only way
for me to be somebody was to be somebody else."
....$250-$450

ROSSO E NERO

ANNO II - N. 8
OTTOBRE - NOVEMBRE 1954
PUBBLICAZIONE MENSILE

• RIVISTA DI ATTUALITA - CINEMA - TEATRO - RADIO - TV •

Sped. in Abb. Post. - Grup. III
Una copia L. 150

Nell'interno

L'INCANTEVOLE LANE
*la nuova Marilyn
inglese*
❖
IL DIVORZIO IN ITALIA
❖
Nuda l'atomica
MARILYN!

Marilyn Monroe

Rosso E Nero. October-November 1954. Italy. Joseph Hepner. The photo on this cover was taken in 1950. Montgomery Clift, who co-starred with Marilyn in *The Misfits*, once had this to say about her: "I have the same problem as Marilyn. We attract people the way honey does bees, but they're generally the wrong kind of people—people who want something from us, if only our energy. We need a period of being alone to become ourselves."

....$80-$125

33

Vue. August 1952. United States. Possibly Joseph Hepner. This cover photo was taken in 1950.
Evidence to the idea that Marilyn wasn't always happy being in the public eye were her own words: "I sometimes feel as if I'm too exposed. I've given myself away, the whole of me, every part, and there's nothing left that's private, just for me alone."
....$50-$80

Tempo. March 8, 1954. United States. Joseph Hepner. This cover photo was taken in 1950. Ever comfortable with the topic of sex at a time when most people weren't so comfortable talking about it, Marilyn once stated, "Nobody ever got cancer from sex." ....$20-$40

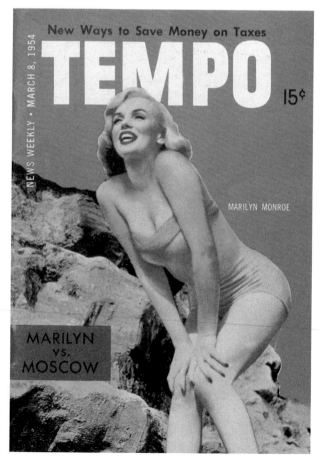

Show. Circa 1955. England. Possibly Joseph Hepner. This cover features a photo of Marilyn taken in 1951. Never one to mince words about how difficult it was for a woman to make her way in Hollywood, Marilyn once said, "You can't sleep your way to being a star...but it helps." ....$60-$100

Focus. March 1953. United States. Unknown. This photo of Marilyn was taken in 1950. That year, Marilyn reported that she did 40 minutes of Calisthenics every day and used 25-pound dumbbells. ....$20-$40

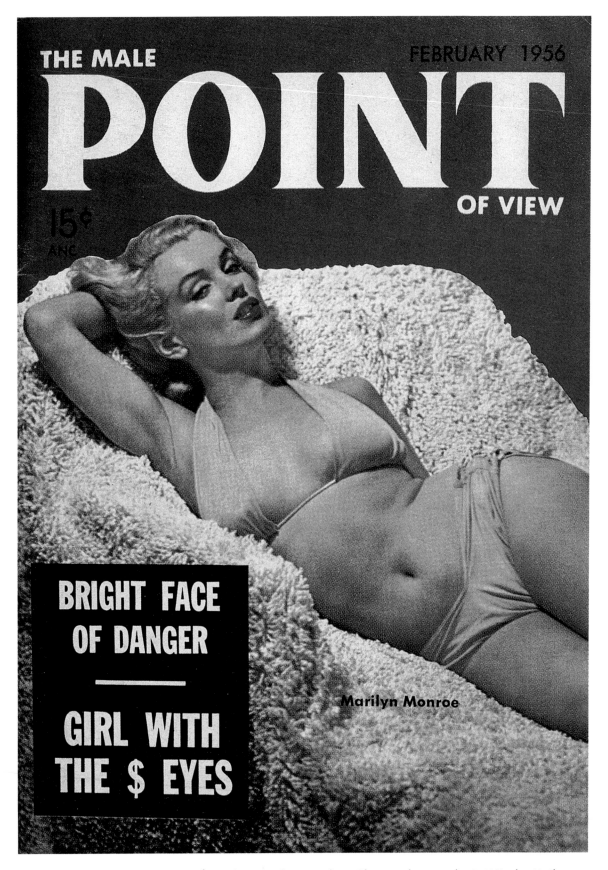

The Male Point of View. February 1956. United States. Anthony Beauchamp. This cover photo was taken in 1951, when Marilyn was still posing for a lot of cheesecake photos. Of those early years, she once said, "It was wonderful being a girl, but it's more wonderful being a woman."

....$20-$40

Eye. August 1953. United States. Anthony Beauchamp. This cover photo was taken in 1950. Marilyn once said: "A woman can bring a new love to each man she loves…providing there are not too many."
....$40-$80

Photography. July 1952. Australia. John Florea. This cover photo was taken in 1951. Another photo from this session was used as a gatefold in *Collier's* magazine that same year. In 1952, Sidney Skolsky asked Marilyn what she wore to bed. Marilyn coyly replied: "Why, Chanel No.5, of course."
....$100-$160

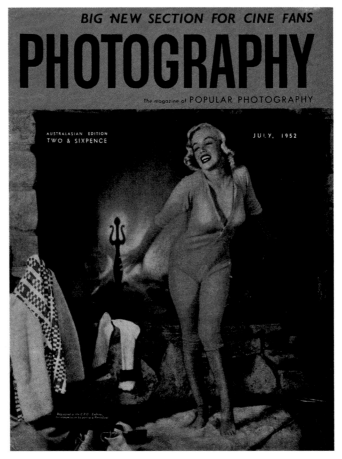

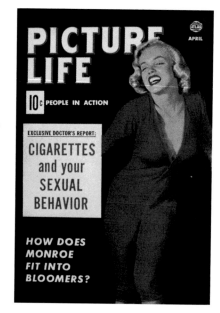

Picture Life. April 1954. United States. John Florea.
This photo of Marilyn was taken in 1951.
The original color of the long-underwear she wore for
this photo was pink. Sometimes equally as unsure
of her own true colors, she said: "Marilyn Monroe has
to look a certain way—be beautiful—and act
a certain way, be talented. I wondered if I
could live up to their expectations."
....$20-$40

Cara Alegre. January 1, 1957. Lisbon. Unknown.
This cover photo was taken in 1951. Marilyn adored all
types of birds and animals, having once said:
"I like animals. If you talk to a dog or a cat,
it doesn't tell you to shut up."
....$40-$70

Billed Bladet. June 26, 1951. Denmark. Unknown.
This cover photo was taken in 1951.
Shortly before her death, Marilyn became very interested
in growing flowers, gardening, and landscaping.
After Marilyn's death, her former housekeeper,
Eunice Murray, counted among her prized possessions a
book on gardening that she had once presented to Marilyn.
....$100-$175

True Story. June 1952. Australia. Don Ornitz. This cover features a photo of Marilyn taken in 1951. She also appeared on the cover of a U.S. issue of *True Story* that year. Hinting at her own "true story," she said, "Being a movie star was never as much fun as dreaming of being one."

....$125-$175

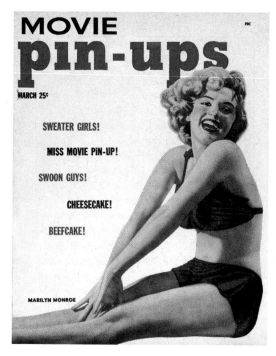

Song Hits Magazine. November 1953. United States. Unknown. This cover features a publicity photo of Marilyn taken in 1951 to promote her roles in *Love Nest* and *As Young As You Feel*. It was reported in one magazine that when Marilyn went to RCA Victor's Hollywood office to negotiate her first recording contract, she said: "I'm so happy to be making records. Now people will get to know another side of me."
....$30-$50

Movie pin-ups. March 1952. United States. Unknown. A rather unflattering image of Marilyn, taken in 1951, graces the cover of this movie magazine. Ever trying to clarify her public persona with the real woman, she said, "A struggle with shyness is in every actor more than anyone can imagine."
....$60-$90

Blighty. January 30, 1954. England. Unknown. Marilyn is shown here serving as hostess at a party thrown in 1951 by Michael Gaszynski, who was known as the cheesecake king of Hollywood. He owned a store called Michael's Cheesecakes.
....$40-$80

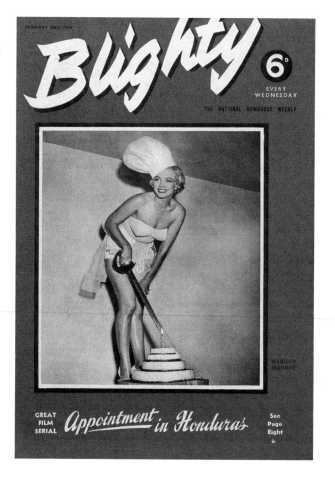

Movie Spotlight. October 1952. United States. Ernest Bachrach. This cover features a publicity photo of Marilyn taken in 1951. Talking candidly about her goals, she said, "As far as I'm concerned, there's a future, and I can't wait to get to it."

....$60-$100

Tempo. October 27, 1951. (Back cover.) Italy. Unknown. Marilyn is seen here with her 35-year-old singing coach, Phil Moore, in 1951. Moore also coached Lena Horne and Dorothy Dandridge. Moore had this to say about Marilyn: "She always sounds as if she's just waking up. You'd be surprised what kind of effect that has on male listeners."

....$40-$80

GOLD COAST
...news magazine...

FREE
TAKE ONE

"YOUR GUIDE TO PLAYCATION LAND"

Gold Coast. October 15, 1952. United States. Unknown. This cover features a publicity photo for *Clash By Night*, taken in October 1951. The magazine proclaims, "What could be more fitting to represent Miami Beach than the way this bathing suit fits Marilyn Monroe?" Paul Douglas, Marilyn's co-star in *Clash By Night*, once watched Marilyn walk away in tight blue denim and cracked, "The end justifies the jeans." ....$80-$120

Funk und Film. May 22, 1954. Germany. Unknown. This cover features a photo of Marilyn taken in 1952. Marilyn was voted "Most Promising Female Newcomer" of 1952 at the *Look* Magazine Achievement Awards. ....$50-$95

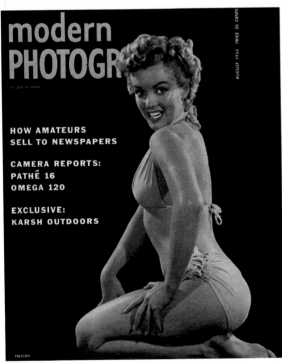

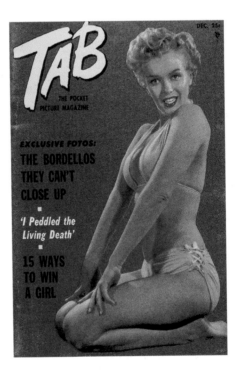

Photo. July 1953. United States. Dave Preston. This cover photo was taken in 1951. Artist Ben Hur Baz based one of his paintings of Marilyn on a photo from this session. That painting was used to grace a calendar in the early 1960s.
....$50-$80

Modern Photography. August 1954. United States. Dave Preston. This cover photo was taken in 1951. Ever a show-stopper in a bikini, Marilyn once said, "If I observed the rules, I'd never have got anywhere."
....$40-$65

Tab. December 1956. United States. Dave Preston. This cover features a 1951 photo of Marilyn. Edward Wagenknecht, author of a book about Marilyn, had this to say after her death: "She was pure of heart. She was free of guile. She never understood either the adoration or the antagonism which she awakened."
....$50-$80

43

RÉVÉLATION

MARILYN MONROE
l'enfant terrible a fait retour
au bercail à Hollywood.
(20 th Century Fox)

N° 3 ★ 40 Francs
Belgique: 6 Frs • Afrique du Nord: 35 Frs
Suisse: 0 F. 50 • Canada: 10 Cents.
Publication Hebdomadaire

Revelation. Circa 1956. France. Ernest Bachrach. This publicity photo of Marilyn was taken in 1951. Marilyn once said, "A photographer once told me that my two best points are between my waist and my neck."

....$100-$150

Tempo. September 13, 1956. Italy. Ernest Bachrach. This photograph of Marilyn was taken in 1951.
....$45-$65

Lecturas. 1953. Spain. Bruno Bernard. This cover features a publicity photo of Marilyn taken in 1951. During a 1952 interview, Marilyn quipped: "Once love let me down— until I came back to earth with a bang. Now I'd rather stay on the ground with a little firmness until I can afford, through experience and security, to walk in the clouds."
....$45-$65

Romantikk. Circa 1952. Norway. Unknown. This 1951 publicity photo for *Clash by Night* shows Marilyn and Keith Andes in embrace. The film was released nationally on June 18, 1952. Marilyn received very good reviews for her performance in the film. During filming, Marilyn bought 25 of her then-famous nude calendars and passed them out to photographers and newsmen on the set. During a 1959 interview with reporter Lou Gerard, Marilyn proclaimed: "My first break was in a picture called *Clash By Night*. Maybe you remember it. I played a dramatic role. I got very good notices. Which doesn't mean that I yearn to be a great dramatic actress. I want to be an actress, which means that I want to be able to play any kind of role capably."
....$40-$90

Picturegoer. November 17, 1956. England. Earl Leaf. Marilyn wore this gown when she accepted the Henrietta Award for "Best Young Box Office Personality" of 1951.
....$30-$40

Romantikk. Circa 1952. Norway. Unknown. Marilyn and Richard Widmark embrace in this publicity photo for the 1952 film *Don't Bother To Knock*. That year, Marilyn was quoted as saying, "I like a part that has something twisted around it."
....$40-$90

Sweetharts. January 1953.United States. Unknown. Marilyn and Richard Widmark grace the cover of this rare comic book in a publicity photo for ***Don't Bother To Knock***. The film was released in the summer of 1952. Of her relationships, Marilyn was clear on one thing: "I was never kept. I always kept myself."

....$100-$200

Cabaret. July 1955. United States. Andre de Dienes. This cover photo was taken in 1952. Marilyn once remarked: "When I was a girl, they called me 'String Bean.' I was so tall in the class pictures, I even had to stand behind the boys. I hated it."
....$40-$75

People Today. July 29, 1953. United States. Gene Kornman. This publicity photo of Marilyn was taken in 1952. That year, Marilyn commented on what she thought about jealousy. She said: "It's like salt on a steak. All you need is a little bit of it."
....$20-$40

Chi e' Marilyn Monroe. June 1, 1954. Italy. Gene Kornman. This cover photo of Marilyn was taken in 1952, and the magazine itself was entirely about Marilyn Monroe. Forever making the censors climb the walls, Marilyn commented on their jobs: "The trouble with censors is they worry if a girl has cleavage. They ought to worry if she hasn't any."

....$150-$275

Picturegoer. August 9, 1952. England. Unknown. This photo was taken in January 1952 while Marilyn was on the set of *We're Not Married*. Dialogue director Tony Jowitt looks on, as Marilyn studies the script for the film. Of acting she often called it "a real struggle. I'm one of the world's most self-conscious people. I really have to struggle."
....$50-$80

8OTTO. March 2, 1952. Italy. Art Adams. This cover features a photo of Marilyn taken in 1952. In 1959, reporter Lou Gerard asked Marilyn what kind of men she considered the sexiest. She replied: "Never thought much about it, but I'll make this distinction: it's a man's inner strength, his spirit, which appeals to me. Women, very much like men, tend to be attracted to the obvious—muscles or good looks. You can include me in, up to a point, on that. But it's that something which doesn't show on the surface which appeals to me. Call it character, or what you will."
....$100-$140

Film Journalen. May 25, 1952. Sweden. Probably Art Adams. This cover gives us a rare behind-the-scenes look at one of Marilyn's photo sessions in 1952.
....$65-$95

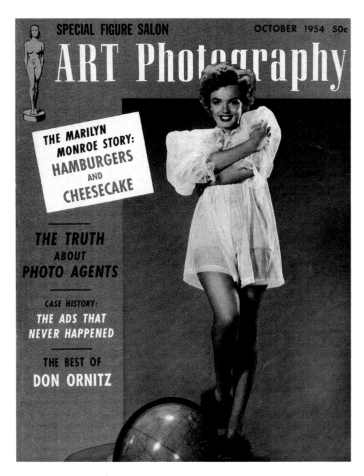

SPECIAL FIGURE SALON   OCTOBER 1954 50c

ART Photography

THE MARILYN
MONROE STORY:
HAMBURGERS
AND
CHEESECAKE

THE TRUTH
ABOUT
PHOTO AGENTS

CASE HISTORY:
**THE ADS THAT
NEVER HAPPENED**

THE BEST OF
DON ORNITZ

Art Photography. October 1954. United States. Unknown. This publicity photo of Marilyn was taken in March 1952. During an interview that year, Marilyn reported that she went for a "jog-trot" every morning dressed variously in blue jeans and a T-neck sweater or a brief suntop. She commented, "The small boys stare at me and shout, 'Who's chasing you?' but I pay no attention to them."
....$40-$60

TV Forecast. October 4, 1952. United States. Culver Pictures. This cover features a publicity photo of Marilyn taken in 1952. Though photographed in many elegant dresses, Marilyn wasn't truly comfortable with dressing up, as she once said: "The worst thing that happens to people when they dress up and go to a party is that they leave their real selves at home."
....$50-$90

All About Imogene Coca • page 6

TV FORECAST

OCTOBER 4, 1952

complete, advance,
TV PROGRAMS

MARILYN MONROE
Banned From Television?

15¢

51

Australasian Post. July 30, 1953. Australia. Unknown. This cover features a publicity photo from 1952, just 10 years before Marilyn's untimely death. After her death in August 1962, *Time* magazine had this to say about Marilyn: "Marilyn Monroe's unique charisma was the force that caused distant men to think that if only a well-intentioned, understanding person like me could have known her, she would have been all right. In death, it has caused women who before resented her frolicsome sexuality to join in the unspoken plea she leaves behind— the simple, noble wish to be taken seriously."
....$50-$90

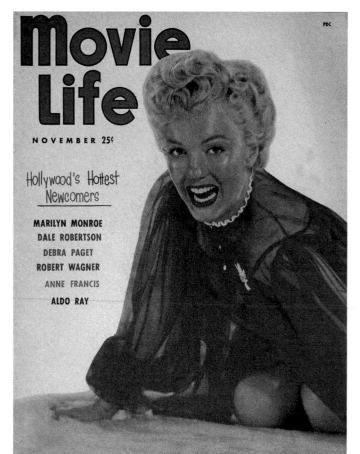

Movie Life. November 1952. United States. Dave Preston. This cover photo of Marilyn was taken in 1952. Marilyn made the following comment that year: "At nights when all the kids were asleep, I'd perch on the dormitory window sill and look across at the RKO water tank with 'RKO' in big letters and light shining like a Hollywood premiere. 'My mother used to work there,' I'd whisper. 'Someday, I'd like to be a star there.'"
....$60-$100

Illustrated. January 31, 1953. England. Bob Landry. This cover features a photo of Marilyn taken in 1952. Labeled on the cover as a "Star Who Startles," Marilyn often startled with her candor on sex, "I sometimes felt I was hooked on sex, the way an alcoholic is on liquor or a junkie on dope." ....$70-$100

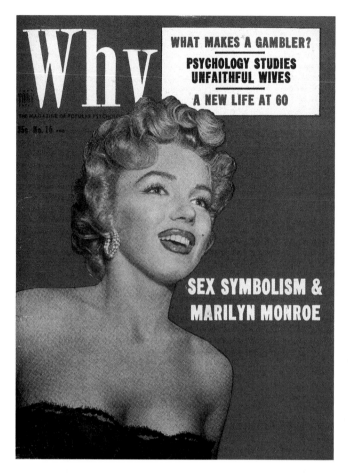

Why. June 1953. United States. Possibly Bob Landry. This cover features a photo of Marilyn taken in 1952. On the downside of being known as a "sex symbol," Marilyn once remarked: "Sometimes I've been to a party where no one spoke to me a whole evening. The men, frightened by their wives or sweeties, would give me a wide berth. And the ladies would gang up in the corner to discuss my dangerous character."
....$40-$60

Hollywood Festival. September 1, 1956. Italy. Unknown. Marilyn is seen here in an interesting publicity photo taken in 1952, just as the 3-D craze was becoming all the rage in America. Hollywood columnist Sheilah Graham once said, "Marilyn's face was covered with a fuzz of downy blond hair which gave her skin a soft, indescribable, luminous quality."
....$65-$125

Picture Roto Magazine. July 27, 1952. United States. Unknown. This cover features a photo of Marilyn taken in the first half of 1952. Marilyn was voted "Cheesecake Queen of 1952" by *Stars and Stripes*.
....$100-$175

Photoplay. January 1953. Australia. Bruno Bernard. This publicity photo of Marilyn was taken in 1952. Marilyn was voted "Fastest Rising Star of 1952" at the *Photoplay* magazine awards held March 9, 1953.

....$60-$100

MARILYN SE SENTAIT TROP SEULE...

Le Soir illustre. August 9, 1962. France. Gene Kornman. The photo of Marilyn on this cover was taken in 1952. Later, famed artist Andy Warhol chose this pose as the subject of one of his now-famous paintings. It was auctioned by Sotheby's in 1998 for $17.3 million.
....$60-$90

Marilyn · Her Tragic Life :
As Joe Saw Her
As Arthur Saw Her
The SEX Symbol
Her Many Loves

200 PICTURES 35,000 WORDS

35¢

Marilyn – Her Tragic Life. 1962. United States. Gene Kornman. This magazine, which was a memorial issue entirely on Marilyn, features a publicity photo taken in 1952. Seeming to foretell her own future, she said: "Yes, there is something special about me, and I knew what it was. I was the kind of girl they found dead in a hall bedroom with an empty bottle of sleeping pills in her hand."
....$40-$80

PHOTOPLAY

October, 1953 1/6

Why the
Stewart Granger
Marriage
Won't Fail

★ PLUS 2 DRAMATIC
TRUE STORIES

Photoplay. October 1953. Australia. Gene Kornman. This publicity photo of Marilyn was taken in 1952. On stardom, she once remarked: "Only the public can make me a star. It's the studios who try to make a system out of it."

....$60-$100

The National Police Gazette. May 1961. United States. Possibly Frank Powolny. The publicity photo on this cover was taken in 1952. Called a "Misfit For Marriage" on this cover, Marilyn seemed to agree when she said: "I've come to love that line 'until death do us part.' It always seems to go well for a time, and then something happens—maybe it's me."

....$25-$45

Vue. January 1955. United States. Frank Powolny. This cover features a publicity photo of Marilyn taken in 1952. That year, Marilyn was quoted as saying, "I've been on all kinds of men's magazine covers, but somehow, I never made the *Ladies' Home Journal*."

....$40-$60

ecran. September 29, 1953. Chile. Frank Powolny. The publicity photo that graces this cover was taken in 1952. Known for her chronic tardiness, Marilyn said, "Being late is a desire not to be there."

....$30-$50

61

The Hotel Dixie Host. December 18, 1954. United States. Frank Powolny. This cover features a 1952 publicity photo. On the matter of romance, she once remarked, "Love is something you can't invent, no matter how much you want to."
....$50-$100

Novella. November 1, 1953. Italy. Frank Powolny. Marilyn graces the cover of this digest-sized magazine in a publicity photo taken in 1952. Photographed so often in beautiful dresses, Marilyn remembered the first one she ever owned herself: "As soon as I could afford an evening gown, I bought the loudest one I could find. It was a bright red, low-cut dress, and my arrival in it usually infuriated half the women present. I was sorry in a way to do this, but I had a long way to go, and I needed a lot of advertising to get there."
....$40-$80

ecran. December 22, 1953. Chile. Frank Powolny. This cover features a publicity photo of Marilyn taken in 1952. The signature and inscription on the cover is not authentic and was probably done by a secretary working in the publicity department at Fox.
....$30-$50

Tempo. August 31, 1953. United States. Possibly Frank Powolny. This cover features a publicity photo of Marilyn from 1952 and makes reference to her romance with Joe DiMaggio. The two were married in January of the following year. Of him, she said: "Joe DiMaggio was the best equipped—the greatest. If our marriage was only sex, it would last forever."
....$20-$40

Movie Stars Parade. December 1954. United States. Ernest Bachrach. This cover features a publicity photo taken in 1952. Ever the lust of every man—married or not—Marilyn realized her effect on the wives when she stated," Wives have a tendency to go off like burglar alarms when they see their husband talking to me."
....$65-$100

Epoca. June 14, 1953. Italy. Ernest Bachrach. This cover features a 1952 publicity photo of Marilyn. Seeming to understand society's view of a woman's place at the time, Marilyn said, "The chief difference between my voice and the voices of most women I've seen is that I use mine less."
....$65-$100

CAVALCADE

JUNE, 1/6   1953

Registered at the G.P.O.,
Sydney, for transmission
by post as a periodical.

You Have a Sixth Sense — page 8

Cavalcade. June 1953. Australia. Ernest Bachrach. The publicity photo of Marilyn on this cover was taken in 1952. After a scandal over Marilyn wearing a low-cut dress that year, she commented, "You would think all other women kept their bodies in vaults."
....$75-$125

Mañana. July 2, 1955. Mexico. Ernest Bachrach. This rare Mexican magazine features a 1952 publicity photo of Marilyn on its cover. During a 1952 interview, Marilyn said, "I don't mind if people *think* I'm a dumb blonde, but I dread the thought of *being* a dumb blonde." ....$60-$100

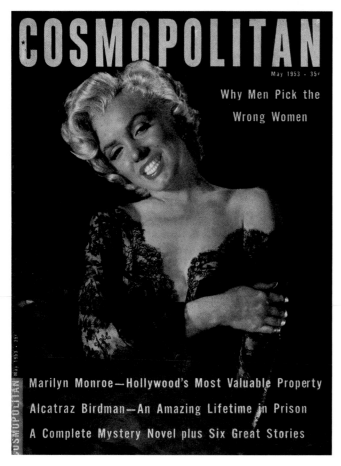

Cosmopolitan. May 1953. United States. Ernest Bachrach. This cover features a publicity photo of Marilyn taken in 1952. Marilyn once commented: "I've given pure sex appeal very little thought. If I had to think about it, I'm sure it would frighten me." ....$75-$125

HOLLYWOOD'S ONE-DAY MIRACLE DIET

MOVIE STARS

MOVIE STARS PARADE/FEBRUARY 25c

PARADE

PDC

the girl
who
rules

MARLON
BRANDO

MARILYN MONROE:
THE NEXT MAN
SHE'LL MARRY

MARILYN MONROE

Ideal
MAGAZINE

Movie Stars Parade. February 1956. United States. Ernest Bachrach. This cover features a 1952 publicity photo. As this cover contemplated what lucky man Marilyn would marry next, a comment she once made about marriage truly revealed how lucky he would be: "I know it's considered chic for a husband and wife to have separate bedrooms, but I'm an old-fashioned girl who believes a husband and wife should share the same bedroom and bed."
....$65-$100

Focus. May 1953. United States. Anthony Beauchamp.
This issue features a series of photos taken in 1952 of Marilyn playing on the beach. Marilyn once commented: "People ask me if I am going on making cheesecake pictures now that I'm a star. My answer is that as long as there is a boy in Korea who wants a pinup of me, I'll go on posing for them."
....$20-$40

Film Stars Album. Winter 1953-54. United States. Unknown.
This cover photo was taken in 1952. Marilyn once said: "Men are like wine—they improve with age. But I don't have nothing against younger men."
....$60-$100

Cahiers Du Cinema. June 1953. France. Unknown.
This cover features a scene still of Marilyn from *Niagara*, taken in 1952. Marilyn once declared, "I'm only comfortable when I'm naked."
....$40-$55

Film Complet. September 17, 1953. France. Unknown. Marilyn is seen embracing her handsome co-star Richard Allen in this scene still from *Niagara*, taken in 1952.

....$40-$65

triunfo. September 30, 1953. Spain. Unknown. Marilyn is seen here in a publicity still for *Niagara*, taken in 1952.

....$50-$80

Kriminal-Roman. October 1953. Germany. Unknown. This cover depicts Joseph Cotton choking Marilyn in a scene still from *Niagara*, taken in 1952. Marilyn once said, "Kindness is the strangest thing to find in a lover—or in anybody."

....$50-$80

69

Family Weekly. February 22, 1959. United States. Bruno Bernard. Marilyn is seen here in a publicity still for *Niagara*, taken in 1952. The film's director, Henry Hathaway, once commented on Marilyn's shower scene in the film: "It's in perfect taste…done on the premise that anticipation is more startling than the real thing. When the males in audiences see Marilyn taking a shower, they'll melt. She can make any move, any gesture, almost insufferably suggestive."

....$55-$100

Piccolo. January 18, 1953. Holland. Bruno Bernard. Marilyn is seen here in a publicity still for *Niagara*, taken in 1952. Speaking of her early acting days, Marilyn once commented: "There were dozens of us on the set, bit players, with a gesture to make and a line or two to recite. Some of them were veteran bit players. After 10 years in the movies, they were still saying one line and walking 10 feet towards nowhere. A few were young and had nice bosoms, but I knew they were different from me. They didn't have my illusions. My illusions didn't have anything to do with being a fine actress. I knew how third-rate I was. I could actually feel my lack of talent, as if it were cheap clothes I was wearing inside. But, my God, how I wanted to learn, to change, to improve! I didn't want anything else—not men, not money, not love, but the ability to act. With the arc lights on me and the camera pointed at me, I suddenly knew myself. How clumsy, empty, uncultured I was; a sullen orphan with a goose egg for a head."
....$55-$100

Tab. August 1955. United States. Bruno Bernard. This cover features a publicity still for *Niagara*, taken in 1952. During an interview in 1952, Marilyn had this to say when the reporter asked her about being known as having "one of the sexiest walks in the business": "You have to walk so that it makes you tingle, and that means you must put enough into it so that you exercise most muscles of the body."
....$40-$65

71

bolero film. July 15, 1956. Italy. Bruno Bernard. This cover photo was taken in 1952. Marilyn is wearing a costume from *Niagara*. On accomplishing her dream to become an actress, she once said: "You don't have to know anything to dream hard. I knew nothing about acting. I had never read a book about it, or tried to do it, or discussed it with anyone. I was ashamed to tell the few people I knew of what I was dreaming." ....$80-$100

Man to Man. June 1956. United States. Bruno Bernard. This cover features a publicity photo, taken in 1952, used to promote Marilyn's role in *Niagara*. The readers of men's magazines like this one probably would have given anything to get some insight into what attracted Marilyn to a particular man, even if what she had to say was more about what she didn't like than what she liked: "The chief drawback with men is that they are too talkative. I don't mean intellectual men who are full of ideas and information about life. It's always a delight to hear such men talk because they are not talking boastfully. The over-talkative men who bore me are the ones who talk about themselves. Sometimes they confine themselves to plain uninterrupted boasting. They'll sit for an hour telling you how smart they are and how stupid everybody else around them is." ....$40-$65

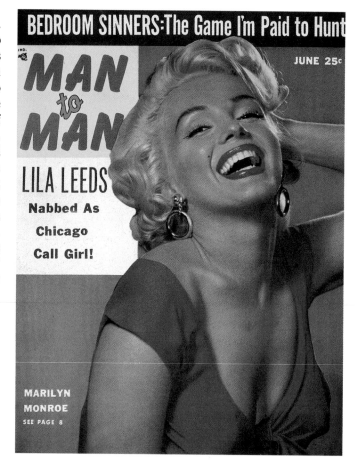

Cine-Revelation. July 19, 1956. France. Bruno Bernard. This cover features a seductive 1952 photo of Marilyn, wearing one of the costumes she wore in *Niagara*. According to Marilyn, there was a trick to looking sexy: "It's easier to look sexy when you are thinking of one man in particular."
....$75-$100

HERREN BEVORZUGEN BLOND
Neue Botschaft aus Hollywood: Marilyn Monroe (siehe „Film")

Der Spiegel. September 30, 1953. Germany.
Robert Cranston and Frank Livia.
This cover features an unretouched photo of Marilyn taken
in 1952 in New York while she was on a tour to promote
Monkey Business. Note the crow's feet around her eyes,
evidence that climbing her way to the top in Hollywood was
no easy task. She once said: "I realized that just as I had
once fought to get into the movies and become an actress, I
would now have to fight to become myself and to be able to
use my talents. If I didn't fight, I would become a piece of
merchandise to be sold off the movie pushcart."
....$60-$90

Screen Stars. July 1955. United States.
Robert Cranston and Frank Livia.
This photo of Marilyn was taken in 1952 on the
aforementioned promotional tour.
During an interview that year, she said:
"I know that some actresses get by for a while
with looks and little else. I don't want to be one of them.
I'd like to carve myself a not-too-large
but permanent niche in the acting world.
In the months and years ahead, I want to learn
everything that is to be learned about acting.
I'll never be a *great* actress, but if I work hard
and believe that what I'm doing is right,
perhaps I can become a *good* one."
....$75-$125

Home and Life Magazine. September 20, 1952. United States. Unknown. Marilyn is seen here arriving at a party thrown in her honor by Ray Anthony in 1952. The party took place at Anthony's home in Sherman Oaks, California. Even Lassie attended!
....$85-$125

Prevue. January 1953. United States. Unknown. This photo of Marilyn was taken at the aforementioned party in 1952.
....$30-$50

Weiner Film Revue. June 20, 1955. Austria. Unknown. Marilyn meets Lassie during the aforementioned party thrown in her honor in 1952. Marilyn had a special place in her heart for animals, perhaps because they could never be as unkind as some of the people she described in the following quote: "Usually they don't say it to me. They say it to the newspapers because that's a bigger play. You know, if they're only insulting me to my face, that doesn't make a big enough play because all i have to do is say, 'See you around, like never.' But if it's the newspapers, it's coast to coast and on around the world. I don't understand why people aren't a little more generous with each other." ....$65-$125

Down Beat. September 10, 1952. United States. Unknown. Marilyn is seen here with composer Ray Anthony. This 1952 photo was used on the sheet music titled "Marilyn," which was a special song written by Anthony especially for Marilyn. ....$35-$70

Music Views. October 1952. United States. Unknown. Marilyn and Ray Anthony perform the song "Marilyn," written by Anthony especially for the aforementioned party at his home. Twenty-three photogphers were present at the 1952 party, and those who worked for *Look* magazine shot pictures from a helicopter!
....$30-$50

Vision. July 24, 1953. Chile. Unknown. Marilyn is seen here at the party thrown in her honor by Ray Anthony in 1952. Actor Mickey Rooney played the drums.
....$75-$125

Wereld Kroniek. February 13, 1954. Holland. Unknown. Marilyn is shown here at Ray Anthony's party thrown in her honor in 1952, an event that was attended by no less than 500 people. Even with so many people who wanted to be around her, Marilyn would always have doubts about being worthy of anyone's love, doubts rooted in a troubled childhood. She once said: "As I grew older, I knew I was different from other children because there were no kisses or promises in life. I often felt lonely and wanted to die. I would try to cheer myself up with daydreams. I never dreamed of anyone loving me as I saw other children loved. That was too big a stretch for my imagination. I compromised by dreaming of my attracting someone's attention (besides God), of having people look at me and say my name."
....$50-$80

Nummer 5. 29 januari — 6 februari 1959. Pris 60 öre

Familje Journalen

Sexig och slagfärdig...

Initierad artikel om Marilyn Monroe

Familje Journalen. January 29- February 6, 1959. Sweden. Unknown. This beautiful candid of Marilyn was taken at the aforementioned party at Ray Anthony's in 1952. Even though she always looked beautiful as the center of attention, Marilyn didn't always like the feeling she got when being scrutinized, once stating: "People had a habit of looking at me as if I were some kind of mirror instead of a person. They didn't see me. They saw lewd thoughts. Then they white-masked themselves by calling me the lewd one."
....$85-$135

ecran. June 29, 1954. Chile. Unknown.
This cover features a publicity photo of Marilyn
taken in about July 1952. The signature and
inscription on the cover are not authentic
and were probably done by a secretary in
the publicity department at Fox.
....$30-$50

Novell Magazinet. Circa 1952. Sweden. Unknown.
Marilyn is featured on this cover in a July 1952
publicity photo. In the September 24, 1952 edition of
Australia's *People* magazine, the following was reported:
"At a recent Los Angeles Press banquet, she (Marilyn)
cornered the cameras by appearing in a bright red,
skin-tight gown of alarming décolletage.
Asked how she got into it, she said,
'I steamed myself for two hours first.
It'll probably have to be cut off.' "
....$30-$50

fotos. June 19, 1954. Spain. Unknown.
This cover photo was taken about July 1952.
Someone other than Marilyn wrote the inscription
shown on this cover, as it is not in her own hand.
At one point in her career, Marilyn was so fed up
with the types of roles she was being offered that she
proclaimed: "I don't want to play sex roles anymore. I'm
tired of being known as the girl with the shape."
....$40-$70

ABC. January 5, 1957. Belgium. Unknown.
Marilyn graces this cover in a publicity photo taken of her
about July 1952. Often quite cynical about men and the way
they had treated her, Marilyn once said, "Most men judge
your importance in their lives by how much you can
hurt them, not by how happy you can make them."
....$40-$65

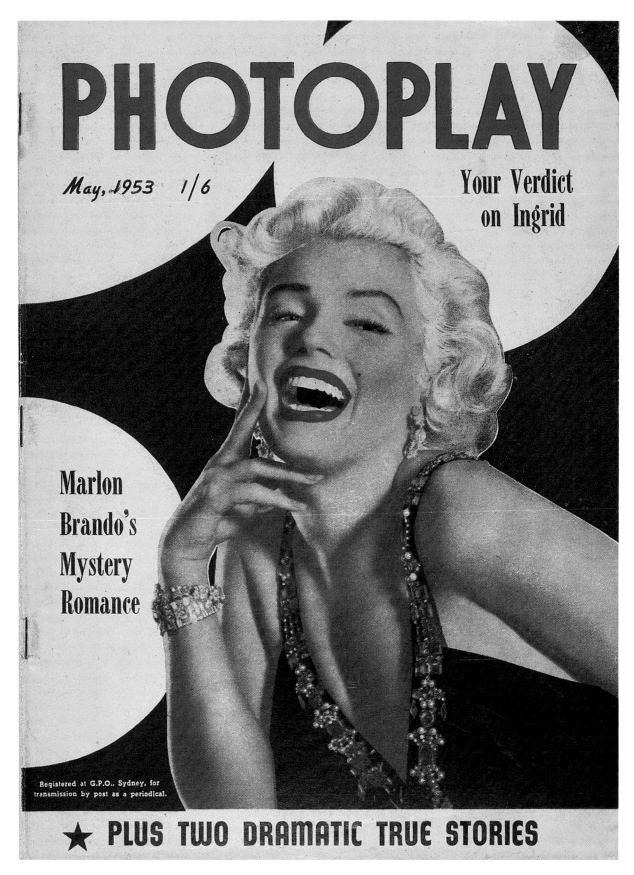

PHOTOPLAY

May, 1953 1/6

Your Verdict
on Ingrid

Marlon
Brando's
Mystery
Romance

Registered at G.P.O., Sydney, for
transmission by post as a periodical.

★ PLUS TWO DRAMATIC TRUE STORIES

Photoplay. May 1953. Australia. Unknown. This cover features a publicity photo of Marilyn taken about July 1952. A sad commentary on how she was sometimes treated in show business: "In Hollywood, they never ask me my opinion. They just tell me what time to come to work."

....$60-$100

Album dos Artistas. No. 2. 1950s. Portugal. Unknown.
This photo was taken about December 1952 and was a costume test for
Marilyn's 1953 film, *Gentlemen Prefer Blondes*.
....$35-$70

Otto Volante. March 16-31, 1953. Italy. Unknown. This cover photo
was taken about January 1953 and was a costume test for *Gentlemen
Prefer Blondes*. A former drama coach of Marilyn's once remembered
her as, "the girl who never raised her hand in class."
....$50-$80

Films in Review. April 1953. United States. Unknown. Marilyn is
seen here reading a copy of the very magazine she is appearing on that
year. The editors of the magazine stated emphatically that it wasn't
staged.
....$100-$150

Cinema. September 30, 1953. Italy. Unknown. Marilyn Monroe and
co-star Jane Russell are shown on this cover in a scene titled "Four
French Dances," which was cut from 1953's *Gentlemen Prefer
Blondes*.
....$40-$65

ANNO VI - N. 9

30 SETTEMBRE
OTTOBRE
★
UNA COPIA L: 150
★
ESCE OGNI MESE

Spedizione da Milano in
abbonam. post. Gruppo III

follie!

MARILYN
MONROE

JANE
RUSSELL

Dal technicolor 20th Century Fox « Gli uomini preferiscono le bionde ».

follie!. September-October 1953. Italy. Unknown. Marilyn and co-star Jane Russell are shown here in a 1953 publicity still for *Gentlemen Prefer Blondes*. When a reporter asked her why she was so outspoken during a 1953 interview, Marilyn proclaimed: "Why shouldn't I speak my mind when I'm asked a lot of questions? Ever since (I was) a kid, I learned to be forthright, honest, and straightforward. Why should I change now?"

....$75-$125

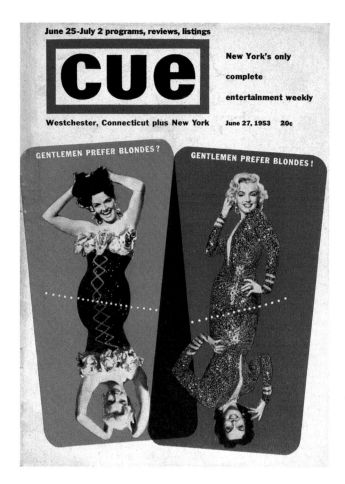

Cue. June 27, 1953. United States. Unknown. Marilyn and Jane Russell are shown here in costumes from the 1953 film *Gentlemen Prefer Blondes*. Always insecure, Marilyn once said: "I went to Glendale tonight and saw a sneak of *Gentlemen Prefer Blondes*. I was awful. I can't act, and I looked hideous. I guess the best thing I can do is just quit and leave town quietly."
....$40-$60

Billed Bladet. May 19, 1953. Denmark. Unknown. Marilyn is seen here in a publicity photo taken in January 1953 for *Gentlemen Prefer Blondes*. Marilyn's measure of a true gentlemen? "When a man says to me, 'I'm giving you exactly the same advice I'd give my own daughter,' I know he isn't 'dangerous' anymore. That is, if he actually has a daughter."
....$50-$90

TV and Movie Screen. November 1953. United States. Unknown. This cover features a publicity still taken in January 1953 for *Gentlemen Prefer Blondes*. The cover queries, "Is Marilyn Monroe Slipping?" Quite a mean-spirited question for a woman so insecure with her acting abilities, evidenced by this comment: "I felt sick. I had told myself a million times that I was an actress. I had practiced acting for years. Here, finally was my first chance at a real acting part with a great director to direct me, and all I could do is stand with quivering knees and a quivering stomach and nod my head like a wooden toy."
....$60-$90

Paris Frou-Frou. Circa 1953. France. Ed Clark. *LIFE* magazine chose this same 1953 publicity photo for *Gentlemen Prefer Blondes* to grace its May 25, 1953 cover.
....$65-$95

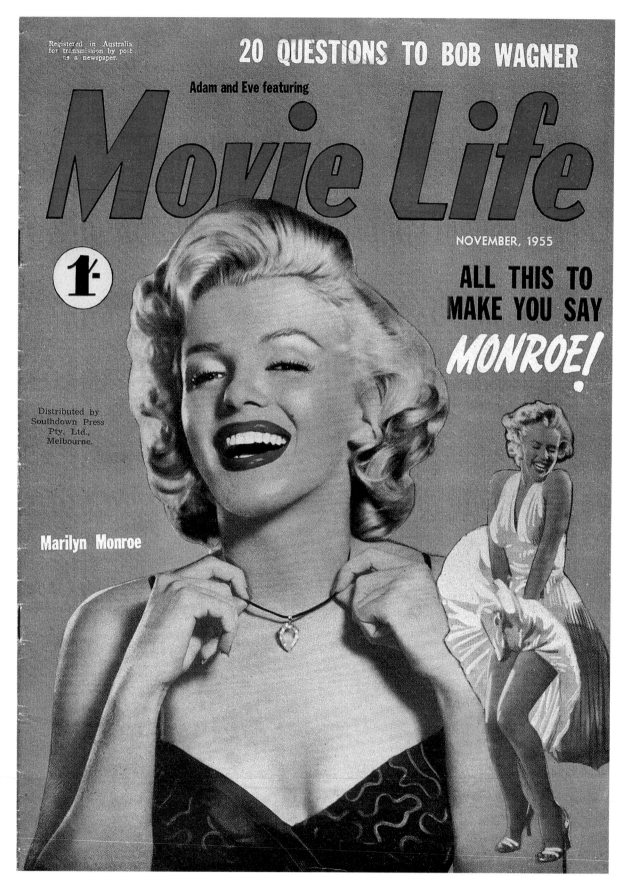

Movie Life. November 1955. Australia. Unknown. This movie magazine features a collage of Marilyn Monroe photos. The main photo, taken in 1953, shows Marilyn wearing a 500-year-old diamond from the collection of Meyer Rosenbaum of Detroit, Michigan.

....$100-$140

"I WAS PAT WARD'S LOVER!"

July 1955   15¢

BEHIND the

SCENE

STANWYCK:
SHE LIKES 'EM YOUNG!

THE 10 MOST
DARING PHOTOS OF
MARILYN MONROE

FLYING SAUCERS FROM EARTH!

Behind the Scene*. July 1955. United States. Unknown. This pocket magazine cover features a publicity photo of Marilyn that was taken in 1953. This cover promises "The 10 Most Daring Photos of Marilyn Monroe," and she clearly had no problem with pushing the envelope, especially where the censors were concerned: "I love to do things the censors won't pass. After all, what are we all here for? Just to stand around and let it pass us by?"
....$20-$40

Uge-Magasinet*. October 1954. Denmark. Unknown. This cover features a 1953 publicity photo. Ever ready to comment on her craft, Marilyn once said: "Acting was something golden and beautiful. It wasn't an art. It was like a game you played that enabled you to step out of the dull world you knew into worlds so bright they made your heart leap just to think of them."
....$40-$70

Uge-Magasinet

NR. 40   25 ØRE

MARILYN MONROE
(FOX FILM)

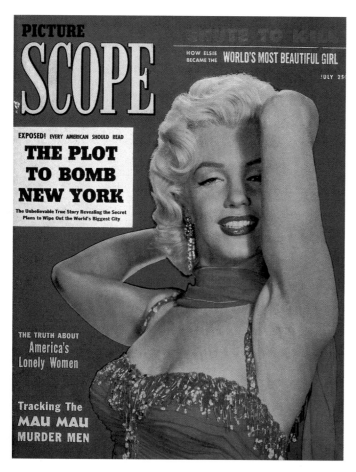

Picture Scope. July 1953. United States. Unknown. This cover features a 1953 photo of Marilyn wearing a costume from *Gentlemen Prefer Blondes*. The photo seems to epitomize this comment she once made about her early quest to be famous: "Some of my foster families used to send me to the movies to get me out of the house, and I'd sit all day and way into the night...I loved anything that moved up there, and I didn't miss anything that happened. I dreamed of myself walking proudly in beautiful clothes and being admired by everyone and overhearing words of praise."
....$75-$100

Confessioni. November 19, 1953. Italy. Frank Powolny. This cover features a 1953 publicity still of Marilyn for *Gentlemen Prefer Blondes*. Artist Franz Kline once said of Marilyn, "She looked like if you bit her, milk and honey would flow from her."
....$50-$80

EPOCA

130 lire - Sett. - 11 agosto 1963
A. XIV - N. 672
Arnoldo Mondadori Editore

A PUNTATE
DA QUESTO NUMERO

RITROVATO L'ALBUM FOTOGRAFICO DI MARILYN MONROE

Epoca. August 11, 1963. Italy. Frank Powolny. Marilyn wore this dress to the *Photoplay* Awards in March of 1953. She was sharply criticized by Joan Crawford for wearing such a low-cut dress. One magazine wrote: "After Joan Crawford ridiculed MM for her low-cut dress…MM was almost in tears… 'What did I do?' she wailed to a friend the next day. 'Sure, I wore a low-cut gown, but so did every other girl in the room. Why does everyone pick on me?'"
....$40-$60

89

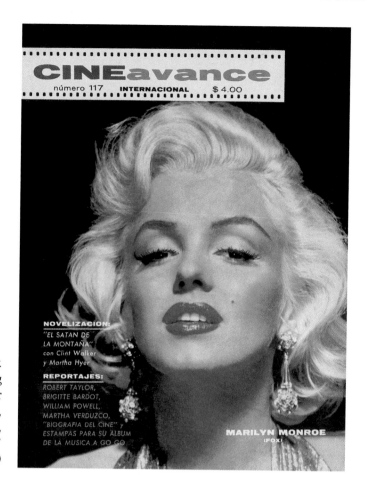

Cine avance. August 10, 1968. Mexico. Frank Powolny. Marilyn is seen in this 1953 publicity photo wearing a gold lamé dress designed by William Travilla for *Gentlemen Prefer Blondes*. Actor Tommy Noonan, referring to kissing Marilyn in that very movie once said, "It was like being sucked into a vacuum."
....$50-$90

L'Europeo. April 13, 1958. Italy. Frank Powolny. This cover features a publicity photo of Marilyn, taken in 1953. During an interview in 1958, Marilyn remarked, "I think a person is made up of a lot of things and as soon as you start nailing it down, you get nowhere."
....$40-$65

Blighty. October 6, 1956. England. Carlyle Blackwell, Jr. This cover features a publicity photo of Marilyn taken in 1953. When asked about her ability to know what got a man's attention, Marilyn once said: "How do I know about man's needs for a sex symbol? I'm a girl!"

....$100-$150

Todo. August 16, 1962. Mexico. Bud Graybell. This rare Mexican magazine features a 1953 image of Marilyn that appears almost airbrushed.
....$125-$175

Gaceta illustrada. May 21, 1960. Spain. John Florea. This cover features a 1953 publicity photo of Marilyn wearing a William Travilla design.
....$100-$150

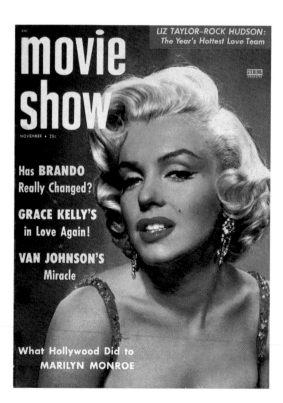

Movie Show. November 1955. United States. John Florea. This cover features a photo of Marilyn taken in 1953, wearing one of her costumes from *Gentlemen Prefer Blondes*.
....$70-$100

92

Pomanteo. 1958. Greece. John Florea.
Marilyn is seen here in one of the dresses she wore in
Gentlemen Prefer Blondes. The photo was taken
in 1953. Always willing to give an opinion on what many
considered too taboo to discuss publicly, Marilyn once said:
"People have curious attitudes about nudity, just as they
have about sex. Nudity and sex are the most commonplace
things in the world, yet people often act as if they were
things that existed on Mars."
....$70-$100

Cinelandia. December 1954. Brazil. Unknown.
This cover features a 1953 publicity photo of Marilyn.
During an interview in her dressing room at Fox,
Marilyn once said: "I'm still trying to find out why I'm here
and what I want. I don't even know what I am. But I'm not
a freak anymore. I've studied hard, and I feel I can act.
Success has many disadvantages. You know, in my early
days in pictures, I left 20th-Fox, or rather, I was let go.
A minor executive tried to get me to go out on his yacht.
When I turned him down—well, we had a battle and I was
fired. But now with success, everyone is very nice to me."
....$50-$80

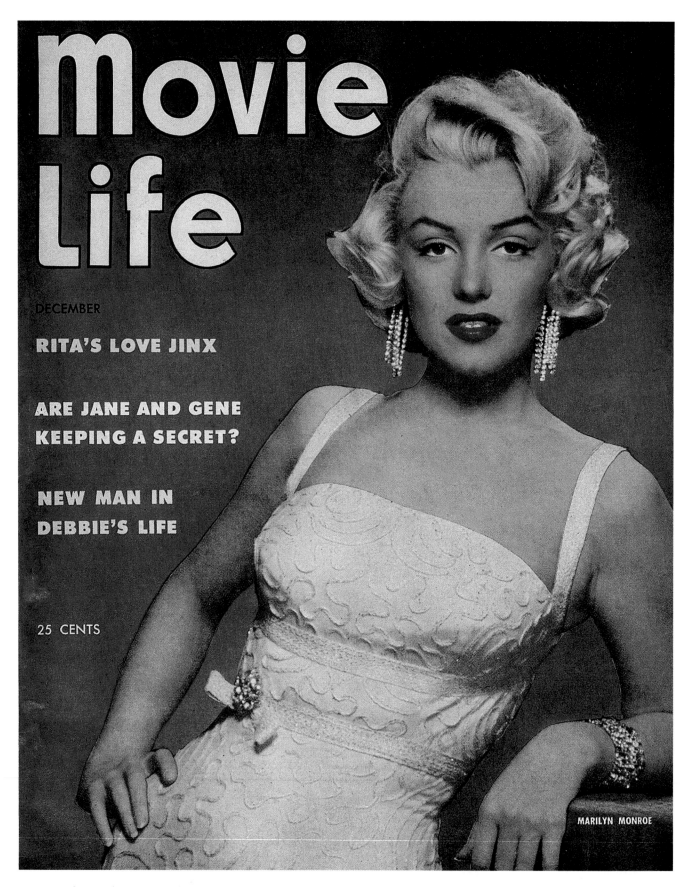

Movie Life

DECEMBER

RITA'S LOVE JINX

ARE JANE AND GENE
KEEPING A SECRET?

NEW MAN IN
DEBBIE'S LIFE

25 CENTS

MARILYN MONROE

Movie Life. December 1953. United States. John Florea. This cover features a publicity photo of Marilyn, taken in 1953. Another glimpse of her insecurity about who she really was became clear when Marilyn said, "I've spent most of my life running away from myself."

....$75-$125

NPOTO. November 24, 1961. Greece. John Florea. This cover features a 1953 publicity photo of Marilyn. Even though she was linked to many powerful men, Marilyn seemed quite high on Ol' Blue Eyes, having said of their romance: "Frank Sinatra is the most fascinating man I ever dated. When I'm with him, I feel like I don't have to take pills."
....$200-$250

Cine Tipo. May 10, 1953. Italy. John Florea. This cover features a publicity photo of Marilyn, taken in 1953. One of Marilyn's biggest disappointments was in never getting to know her father, especially given her mother's emotional instability. She remembered: "Whenever I visited my mother, I would stand looking at this photograph (of her father) and hold my breath for fear she would order me to stop looking. I had found out that people always ordered me to stop doing anything I liked to do."
....$75-$125

Tempo. December 27, 1955. United States. John Florea. This cover features yet another publicity photo of Marilyn taken in 1953, this time in a negligee, second-best in Marilyn's opinion to posing nude: "My impulse to appear naked and my dreams about it had no shame or sense of sin in them. Dreaming of people looking at me made me feel less lonely. I think I wanted them to see me naked because I was ashamed of the clothes I wore— the never-changing faded blue dress of poverty. Naked, I was like the other girls and not someone in an orphan's uniform."
....$20-$40

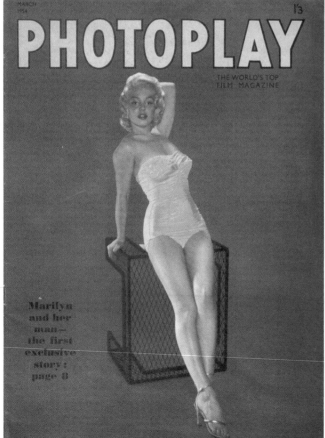

Photoplay. March 1954. England. Frank Powolny. This cover features a 1953 publicity photo of Marilyn. Speaking about when she came to realize that she might be pretty, Marilyn remembered when she was 11 years old: "Suddenly, everything opened up. Even the girls paid a little attention to me just because they thought, 'Hmm, she's to be dealt with.'"
....$40-$80

MOVIES

JUNE 25¢

PDC
Ideal
MAGAZINE

DON'TS FOR MY DAUGHTER

by June Allyson

MY KIND OF LOVE
by Tony Curtis

UNTOLD FACTS
about Rory Calhoun

Doris Day:
SERVICEMEN'S DELIGHT

Special TV SECTION:
JULIUS LA ROSA
DINAH SHORE
JO STAFFORD
JACK WEBB

MARILYN MONROE

Movies. June 1954. United States. Unknown. This cover features a 1953 publicity photo of Marilyn in which she is wearing a costume from *How to Marry a Millionaire*.
....$65-$95

Illustrated. August 8, 1953. England. Earl Theisen. This cover features a 1953 publicity photo of Marilyn, with co-stars Betty Grable and Lauren Bacall for *How to Marry a Millionaire*. Actress Shelley Winters once had this to say about Marilyn: "She'd come out of our apartment in a shleppy old coat, looking like my maid, and all the people would push her aside to get my autograph. She loved it."
....$50-$90

New Screen News. February 12, 1954. Australia. Probably Earl Theisen. This cover depicts Marilyn in a publicity photo for *How to Marry a Millionaire*, taken in 1953.
....$40-$65

Tempo. December 17, 1953. Italy. Earl Theisen. This cover depicts a 1953 publicity photo for *How to Marry a Millionaire*, featuring Marilyn with co-stars Betty Grable and Lauren Bacall.
....$35-$50

Mimosa. January 1955. Italy. Unknown. Marilyn is seen here, along with co-stars Betty Grable and Lauren Bacall, clowning around on the set of *How to Marry a Millionaire* in 1953. Marilyn once said, "I strove to look like Betty Grable, but thought Alice Faye had more class to her looks."

....$40-$65

Min Melodi. 1953. Sweden. Unknown. This cover depicts a photo of Marilyn, along with co-stars Betty Grable and Lauren Bacall, on the set of *How to Marry a Millionaire* in 1953. After Marilyn's death in 1962, Betty Grable had this to say about Marilyn: "It may sound peculiar to say so, because she is no longer with us, but we were very close. Once when we were doing that picture together, I got a call on the set; my younger daughter had had a fall. I ran home and the one person to call was Marilyn. She did an awful lot to boost things up for movies when everything was at a low state. There'll never be anyone like her for looks, for attitude, for all of it."

....$50-$80

Cine Revue. April 12, 1957. France. Unknown. This cover features a publicity photo of Marilyn, taken in 1953. Remembering the time when she realized she had "made it," Marilyn said: "I really got the idea I must be a star, or something, from the newspapermen—I'm saying men not women—who would interview me and they would be warm and friendly. By the way, that part of the press, you know, the men of the press, unless they have their own personal quirks against me, they were always very warm and friendly and they'd say, 'You know, you're a star,' and I'd say, 'Star?' and they'd look at me as if I were nuts. I think they, in their own kind of way, made me realize I was famous."

....$30-$40

Screen-Radio-Television. September 6, 1953.
United States. Frank Powolny.
This cover features a 1953 publicity photo.
....$100-$175

Cinemonde. May 10, 1960. Unknown.
This cover features a publicity photo of Marilyn,
taken in 1953. Responding to criticism that she wasn't
always truthful, Marilyn once said: "When I talk, I have
a bad habit of not finishing sentences, and this gives
the impression I'm telling lies. I'm not. I'm just not
finishing sentences."
....$40-$60

RADIO REVUE

DIE PROGRAMM-ZEITSCHRIFT FÜR JEDEN
NR. 39 · VOM 27. SEPT. BIS 3. OKT. 1953

30 Pf.

Im Abonnement 25 Pf.
zuzüglich Zustellgeld
Verlagsort Berlin

Das Mädchen, das nicht lieben konnte . . . so heißt unser neuer Roman, mit dessen Abdruck wir in diesem Heft beginnen. Aber dieses Mädchen hier, Marilyn Monroe, verführerisch schön, ist in dem Film „Niagara" eher das Gegenteil unserer Romanheldin. Foto: 20th Century-Fox

Radio Revue. September 27-October 3, 1953. Germany. Unknown. This cover features a publicity photo of Marilyn, taken in 1953.
....$50-$90

Wereld Kroniek. June 23, 1956. Holland. Probably Frank Powolny. Another 1953 publicity shot is featured on this cover.
....$40-$70

Hollywood Festival. October 17, 1953. Italy. Frank Powolny. This cover features a publicity photo of Marilyn, taken in 1953. At one point, Marilyn talked about her life as Norma Jeane as though that girl had died and been replaced: "This is the end of my story of Norma Jeane. I moved into a room in Hollywood to live by myself. I was 19, and I wanted to find out who I was."
....$35-$70

Illustrierte Film Kurier. March 1954.Germany. Frank Powolny (main photo). This cover features a composite of images of Marilyn, all taken in 1953. Of the difficulty in trying to find acting opportunities when one first decides to pursue a movie career, Marilyn once made the analogy, "A movie job hunter without a care in Hollywood is like a fireman without a fire engine."
....$35-$70

Hafta. September 1957. Turkey. Bert Reisfeld. This cover features a 1953 publicity photo. When it came to falling in love, Marilyn had some interesting insights, like the time she said, "It is hard to explain how much you can fall in love while you are being bored to death, but I know it's true, because it happened to me several times."
....$40-$70

Tabarin. March 1954. Italy. Bert Reisfeld. This cover photo was taken in 1953. That same year, Marilyn was voted "World Film Favorite" at the Golden Globe Awards.
....$40-$75

Le Ore. August 1, 1953. Italy. Bert Reisfeld. This cover features a publicity photo of Marilyn, taken in 1953. That year, columnist Henry McLemore said, "A lady from way back…quiet, gentle, gracious, and the sort of girl you'd like to bring home and say, 'Mama, this is Marilyn.' "
....$50-$70

TV. September 1955. United States. Bert Reisfeld. This cover features a 1953 publicity photo of Marilyn, along with photos of Nanette Fabray, Eva Marie Saint, and Gail Davis.
....$25-$40

Paris Match. July 25, 1953. France. Possibly Bert Reisfeld. This cover features a 1953 publicity photo of Marilyn. Publicist Roy Craft once said, "She had such magnetism that if 15 men were in a room with her, each man would be convinced he was the one she'd be waiting for after the others left."
....$70-$95

3-D Star pin-ups. December 1953. United States. Possibly Bert Reisfeld. This cover features a 1953 publicity photo of Marilyn. 3-D was all the rage in 1953. Marilyn is seen here on one of three 3-D magazine covers she appeared on. The magazines came with a pair of 3-D glasses bound inside.
....$90-$125

Le Ore. October 9, 1954. Italy. Bert Reisfeld.
This cover features a 1953 publicity photo of Marilyn.
William Travilla, who designed many of the costumes
Marilyn wore in her films, once had this to say about
Marilyn: "On the surface, she was still a happy girl. But
those who criticized her never saw her as I did, crying like
a baby because she often felt herself so inadequate."
....$45-$65

Le Ore. June 21, 1958. Italy. Bert Reisfeld.
This cover features a 1953 publicity photo of Marilyn.
During an interview in 1958, Marilyn talked about still
being recognized immediately when going out, but the fans
were not responding with "the same sense of urgent
excitement." She commented: "You come to expect a
certain kind of reaction, even though it can be a nuisance.
But when it isn't there, or when it's modified, you
experience a kind of pang. After all, it's what you've
worked for so hard all of these years."
....$40-$65

Neue Illustrierte. July 25, 1953. Germany. Possibly Bert Reisfeld. This cover features a 1953 publicity photo of Marilyn.
....$90-$125

Cine Radio Actualidad. December 25, 1953. Uruguay. Possibly Bert Reisfeld. This cover features a 1953 publicity photo. Marilyn once commented on her early days in foster homes: "…and when Christmas came, it was always different for me. The families would buy us all dresses, maybe, but I'd get the brown one or the cheapest one. And one year, all the other kids in the family I lived with got wonderful presents, and I got a 10-cent manicure outfit. And while the rest of the kids sat around the floor and admired their loot, I sat in a corner pushing back my cuticle. Yes, the Christmases were the hardest."
....$40-$65

Manchete. August 1962. Brazil. Unknown. This photo of Marilyn was taken in May 1953 while Marilyn was attending a birthday party for TV commentator and syndicated columnist Walter Winchell. The party was thrown by the Los Angeles Press Club at Ciro's in Hollywood.
....$70-$100

REVISTA DE
AMERICA

MEXICO, D. F., MARZO 4 DE 1961   No. 793

MARILYN MONROE

$1.00

Revista De America. March 4, 1961. Mexico. Unknown. This rare magazine features a photo of Marilyn taken at a Hollywood party in May 1953.
....$125-$175

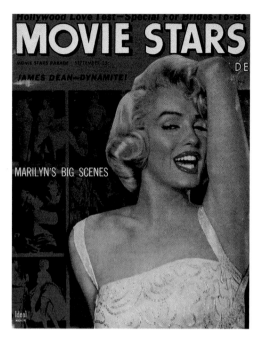

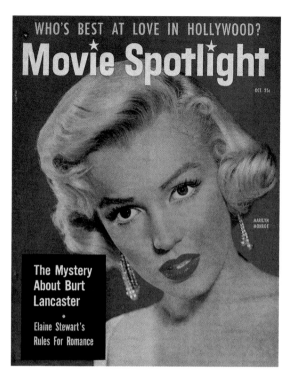

Movie Stars Parade. September 1955. United States. Unknown.
This cover features a 1953 publicity photo. Marilyn once remarked:
"Friends are so important. You bounce ideas and thoughts off them
and learn more about yourself. My friends are such that I know if I
weren't a person of some substance, they wouldn't have anything
to do with me."
....$60-$95

Movie Spotlight. October 1954. United States. Unknown.
This cover features a 1953 publicity photo of Marilyn. Sammy Davis, Jr.
said after Marilyn's death, "Still she hangs like a bat in the heads of
the men who met her, and none of us will ever forget her."
....$65-$95

ecran. December 1960. Chile. Unknown. This cover features a 1953
publicity photo. Of the need not to have to publicize when she was
available, Marilyn once said, "When you don't want a lover, all kinds
of opportunities come your way."
....$30-$40

110

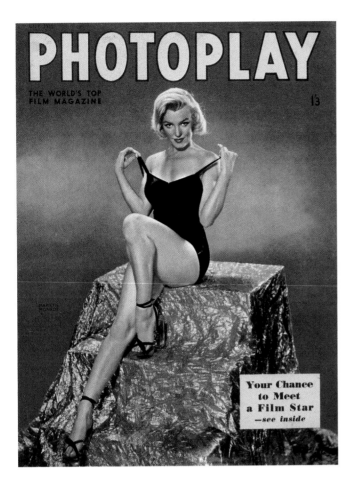

Photoplay. July 1955. England. John Florea.
This cover features a 1953 publicity photo of Marilyn.
In July 1955, Marilyn proclaimed: "I've fallen in love
with Brooklyn. I'm going to buy a little house in Brooklyn
and live there. I'll go to the coast only when I have to make
a picture."
....$40-$65

Focus. January 1955. United States. Frank Powolny.
A 1953 publicity photo graces this cover. In 1955, Marilyn
proclaimed: "I feel wonderful. I'm incorporated."
She was referring to her newly formed company,
Marilyn Monroe Productions.
....$20-$40

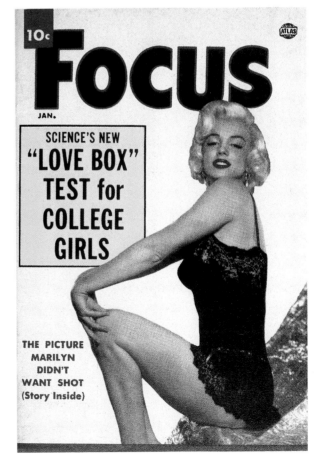

111

ANC

INSIDE HOLLYWOOD
ANNUAL

25¢

**DEBBIE
and EDDIE:
Is their love
in danger?**

**ROCK HUDSON:
The truth about
that "mystery
woman"**

MARILYN MONROE

Inside Hollywood Annual. 1955. United States. Frank Powolny. This cover features a publicity photo of Marilyn, taken in 1953. Of her tastes in men, Marilyn once said, "I've always been attracted to men who wore glasses."

....$60-$90

20th Century Fox. February 28, 1954. Italy. Frank Powolny. Marilyn is seen here in a 1953 publicity photo. Reflecting on a life that was not easy before stardom, Marilyn once said, "The dark star I was born under was going to get darker and darker." ....$50-$80

Picture Scope. May 1955. United States. Frank Powolny. This cover features a cheesecake-type publicity photo taken in 1953. Marilyn posed for very few cheesecake photos after 1953. ....$40-$65

Se. May 1958. Sweden. Milton H. Greene. This photo of Marilyn was taken in 1953 at the base of a scabrous cliff in Laurel Canyon. ....$40-$70

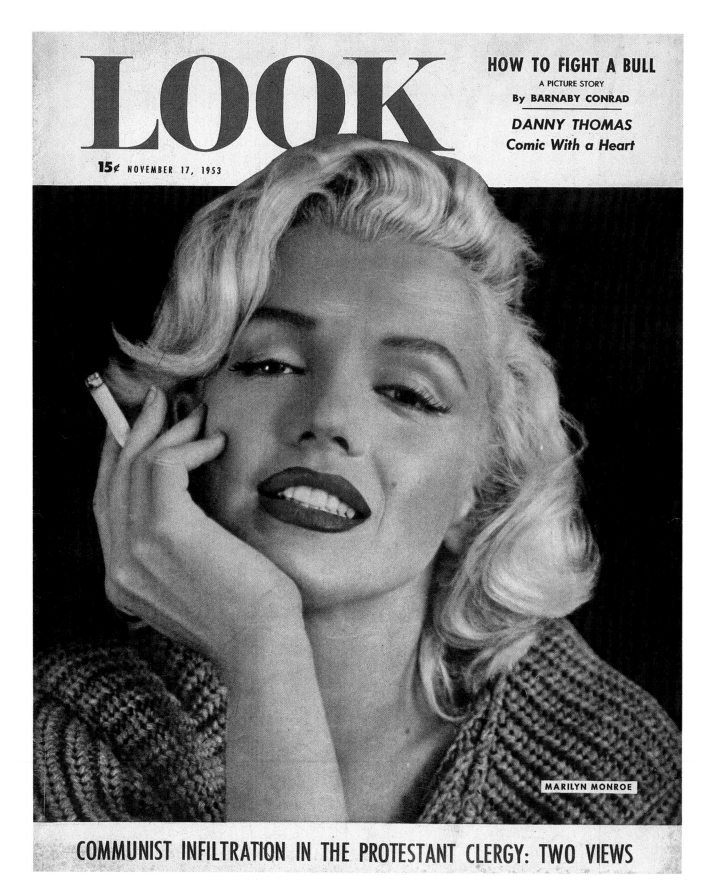

LOOK

15¢ NOVEMBER 17, 1953

HOW TO FIGHT A BULL
A PICTURE STORY
By BARNABY CONRAD

DANNY THOMAS
Comic With a Heart

MARILYN MONROE

COMMUNIST INFILTRATION IN THE PROTESTANT CLERGY: TWO VIEWS

Look. November 17, 1953. United States. Milton H. Greene. Milton Greene first met Marilyn in 1953, and this cover shot was taken that year, in one of the very first photo sessions he had with Marilyn.

....$60-$100

Visto. July 10, 1954. Italy. Milton H. Greene. This cover photo was taken in 1953. Milton Greene and Marilyn became close friends, and eventually business partners in Marilyn Monroe Productions. Shortly after Marilyn's marriage to Arthur Miller, the partnership was dissolved. Greene took some of the most beautiful photos ever taken of Marilyn. ....$80-$125

Pleasure. Australia. Circa 1964. Unknown. This cover photo was taken in August 1953 while Marilyn was on location in Banff, Alberta, Canada filming *River of No Return*, which co-starred Robert Mitchum and Rory Calhoun. ....$25-$45

Movie Life Year Book. 1954. United States. Unknown. This cover photo was taken in August 1953 while Marilyn was on location in Canada to film *River of No Return*. . . . .$40-$65

Bold. January 1954. United States. John Vachon. This cover features a photo of Marilyn Monroe and Joe DiMaggio taken while they were dating during the filming of *River of No Return* in late-1953. Marilyn met Joe on a blind date in 1952. A romance ensued, and the couple was married in a modest ceremony in San Francisco on January 14, 1954. The marriage lasted only nine months.
....$20-$40

Photoplay. December 1954. England. Bruno Bernard. This cover features a publicity photo of Marilyn taken in August or September 1953. Marilyn wore this costume during one of her song-and-dance numbers in *River of No Return*.
....$40-$80

TV life. January 1954. United States. Probably Frank Powolny. This cover features another 1953 publicity photo for *River of No Return*. In 1954, one magazine reported that columnist Mike Connolly called Marilyn "the most insecure person in Hollywood."
....$20-$40

cine fan. December 1957. Brazil. Probably Frank Powolny. This cover features a 1953 publicity photo of Marilyn for *River of No Return*. When asked about the film, Marilyn said: "Knowing what I know now, I wouldn't accept *River of No Return*. I think I deserve a better deal than a 'Z' cowboy movie, in which the acting finishes third to the scenery and Cinemascope."

....$50-$90

117

Romantikk. Circa 1954. Norway. Probably Frank Powolny. Marilyn and co-star Rory Calhoun embrace in this publicity photo for *River of No Return*, taken in 1953.
....$35-$70

TV sorrisi e canzoni. July 11, 1954. Italy. Probably Frank Powolny. This cover depicts Marilyn with co-star Robert Mitchum in a 1953 publicity still for *River of No Return*.
....$60-$90

Cine Radio Actualidad. October 15, 1954. Uruguay. Unknown. This cover is a composite. Marilyn's photo has been superimposed over a selection of magazine covers that she had graced. The photo of Marilyn was taken at the premiere of *How to Marry a Millionaire* in 1953.
....$40-$60

Luke-Mista Kaikille. 1955. Finland. Frank Powolny. A 1953 publicity photo graces this cover. Marilyn once had this to say about Los Angeles: "Even though I was born there, I still can't think of one good thing to say about it. If I close my eyes and picture L.A., all I see is one big varicose vein."
....$40-$70

119

Estudio. May 5, 1954. Portugal. Frank Powolny. This cover features a publicity photo taken in 1953. Marilyn once remarked: "Flashy earrings, necklaces, and bracelets detract from a lady's looks. And even if I have to wear that stuff, I don't have to own it. The studio loans it to me whenever they want to show me off."

....$100-$140

O Seculo Ilustrado. January 30, 1954. Portugal. Unknown. This cover features a photo of Marilyn and her new husband, Joe DiMaggio, taken on their January 14, 1954 wedding day. Shortly before Marilyn's marriage to Joe, she was receiving 5,000 marriage offers a week from her adoring male fans! DiMaggio's ex-wife Dorothy Arnold sought a court order to keep Joe from taking Joe, Jr. to visit Marilyn, where "liquor was plentiful, and other children infrequent." When interviewed about the incident, Marilyn told a reporter, "I want to love and be loved more than anything else in the world."
....$30-$60

Oggi. January 28, 1954. Italy. Unknown. This cover features a photo of the newlyweds, Joe DiMaggio and Marilyn Monroe, taken on their wedding day of January 14, 1954. After Marilyn's divorce, her make-up man Alan Snyder made this comment: "Joe DiMaggio may not have made a good husband for Marilyn, but no one cared more for her. He was always—before the divorce and after the divorce—her best friend."
....$30-$50

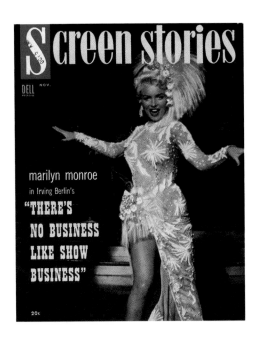

Screen stories. November 1954. United States. Unknown. Marilyn is shown here in a scene still for *There's No Business Like Show Business*, taken in 1954. The dress was designed by William Travilla. The film did not do well at the box office, and Marilyn's marriage to Joe DiMaggio had begun to crumble during filming.
....$40-$65

Estudio. November 20, 1955. Portugal. Unknown. Marilyn takes a break on the set of *There's No Business Like Show Business* in 1954. Co-star Donald O'Connor is on the left.
....$35-$70

Mein Film. January 1955. Austria. Unknown. Marilyn Monroe and Donald O'Connor are featured on this cover in a 1954 publicity photo for *There's No Business Like Show Business*.
....$40-$65

Film Magazin. January 4, 1955. Switzerland. Bruno Bernard. This cover features a 1954 publicity photo of Marilyn used to promote *There's No Business Like Show Business*.
....$40-$70

Billed Bladet. October 11, 1957. Denmark. Unknown. Marilyn is shown here leaning out an apartment window in New York in 1954. She was on location filming scenes for *The Seven Year Itch*.
....$50-$90

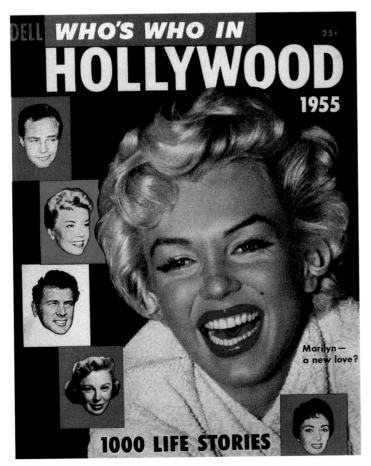

Who's Who in Hollywood. 1955. United States. Unknown. This cover features a photo of Marilyn taken on location during the filming of *The Seven Year Itch* in New York City in September 1954. She was leaning out an apartment window when this shot was taken.
....$40-$65

TV France. August 18-24, 1962. France. Unknown. Marilyn is seen here in a photo taken during the filming of *The Seven Year Itch* in 1954. Marilyn once remarked: "I'm happy where I am now (New York). Happiness is something I'm sort of scared to talk about. I'm superstitious about it. But I'll never return to Hollywood to live. This is my home forever and ever!"

....$60-$90

Gente. August 31, 1966. Italy. Unknown. Marilyn is seen here during a night out at the Hollywood Stork Club with Joe DiMaggio in 1954, while Marilyn was on location to shoot scenes for *The Seven Year Itch*. The club was located at 3 East 53rd Street in New York.
....$30-$50

Action. October 1954. United States. Unknown. This cover photo was taken when Marilyn helped celebrate the first anniversary of Cinemascope in 1954. She is wearing the famous dress from *The Seven Year Itch*.
....$50-$85

125

Visioni. May 14, 1955. Italy. Unknown. In the wee hours of a September 1954 morning, Marilyn shot a scene for ***The Seven Year Itch***
at 52nd Street and Lexington Avenue in New York. There were dozens of photographers on the scene, in addition to several thousand
onlookers, including Joe DiMaggio with his friend, columnist Walter Winchell. Although she wore two pairs of underwear, the bright lights
revealed a little too much for Joe to handle. As the dress blew higher and higher, so did Joe's temper. He stormed off, and later he and
Marilyn got into a very heated argument over the event.
....$90-$120

Cine Radio Actualidad. September 16, 1955. Uruguay. Unknown.
This cover features the famous skirt-blowing scene from
The Seven Year Itch, which was featured on covers the
world over. The photo session took place in September 1954.
Billy Wilder, who directed Marilyn in *Itch*, once said of her:
"She's scared and unsure of herself. I found myself wishing that
I were a psychoanalyst and she were my patient.
It might be that I couldn't have helped her,
but she would have looked lovely on a couch."
....$25-$50

Fotogramas. October 15, 1954. Spain. Unknown.
This cover shows Marilyn, with her attorney Jerry Geisler
at her side, announcing her divorce from Joe DiMaggio on
October 4, 1954. The announcement was made from the
front lawn of their home in Beverly Hills.
....$40-$70

CORREO DE LA RADIO

REVISTA NACIONAL DE RADIODIFUSIÓN ● MADRID - BARCELONA

N.º 38 ● AGOSTO 1955 ● PRECIO: CINCO PESETAS

Correo De La Radio. August 1955. Spain. Unknown. This cover features a publicity photo taken in 1954 to promote *The Seven Year Itch*, which was released in 1955. During an interview in 1959, reporter Lou Gerard asked Marilyn if she would like to be remembered in the distant future as "America's symbol of sex." She replied: "If that's the best I can do, then the answer is yes. If you're remembered for anything, you've been a success, haven't you?"

....$60-$100

Oggi. October 21, 1954. Italy. Unknown.
This cover features a photo of Marilyn with director
Billy Wilder, taken while filming *The Seven Year Itch*
in 1954. Marilyn once said, "A career is wonderful,
but you can't curl up with it on a cold night."
....$30-$50

Vie Nuove. May 18, 1957. Italy. Frank Powolny.
This cover features a publicity still of Marilyn taken in
1954 to promote *The Seven Year Itch*, released in 1955.
During a 1959 interview, reporter Lou Gerard made
Marilyn laugh when he told her there were rumors that
she might quit making movies. She replied:
"It's never occurred to me. I'll never again make
three or four pictures a year, of course. Apart from the
tremendous amount of work involved, there's the
matter of too much exposure to audiences."
....$50-$85

Flix. Circa 1955. England. Unknown.
This cover features a publicity photo taken in 1954
to promote *The Seven Year Itch*. Marilyn once said:
"I've never said I won't make pictures for 20th Century-Fox.
I think *The Seven Year Itch* is the best picture I've ever
made. I loved working with Billy Wilder, and I learned a lot
from him. I need somebody to help me, and he gave me
great help. I want to make musicals, good comedies, and
drama—not (just) heavy drama as everyone says."
....$60-$100

129

Flix. Circa 1955. England. Unknown. This cover features a publicity photo of Marilyn and co-star Tom Ewell taken in 1954 to promote *The Seven Year Itch*. Referring to Marlene Deitrich as a grandmother, Marilyn once told a reporter, "That's the only true kind of sex appeal—when men find you fascinating and desirable even though your youth is gone." ....$60-$100

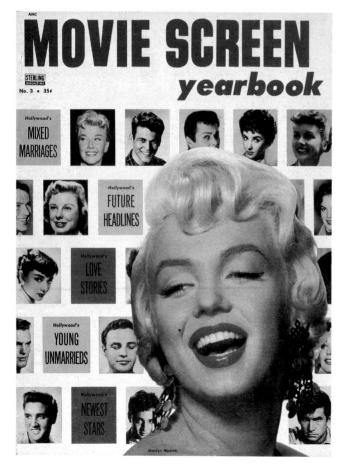

Movie Screen yearbook. 1957. United States. Frank Powolny. This cover depicts a publicity still taken in 1954 to promote *The Seven Year Itch*. Marilyn once told a reporter: "Sex appeal in movies—especially because of those close-ups—is based purely on the surface aspects. When the bloom is off the rose, and the camera can't hide the encroaching years, you've got to have that something else I mentioned, or you're all washed up." ....$50-$80

New
SCREEN NEWS

Registered at G.P.O., Melbourne for transmission by post as a newspaper.

Vol. 9, No. 22

NOVEMBER 4, 1955

6ᴰ

MARILYN MONROE
and
TOM EWELL

New Screen News. November 4, 1955. Australia. Unknown. This magazine was handed out in the lobby of movie theaters in Australia. The cover depicts Marilyn and her co-star Tom Ewell in a publicity photo taken in 1954 to promote *The Seven Year Itch*, which was released in 1955.
....$40-$60

Le Film Complet. May 1956. France. Unknown. Marilyn and co-star Tom Ewell embrace on this cover in a publicity photo taken in 1954 to promote *The Seven Year Itch*. When quizzed by a reporter about why she applies much of her own make-up, Marilyn proclaimed, "If Dietrich knows the best side of her leg, I should know the best side of my face."
....$40-$60

L'Europeo. December 4, 1955. Italy. Ted Baron Studios. Ted Baron was also a court photographer. This cover photo was taken in late-1954. Commenting on her fame, Marilyn once said: "All that I knew was that I didn't care about money. I just wanted to be wonderful."
....$40-$80

Le Ore. June 4, 1955. Italy. Ted Baron Studios. This cover photo was taken in late-1954. When Marilyn was asked what her future plans were in the mid-1950s, she replied: "I have no big plans. I like Hollywood, and I'll make a picture from time to time and try to learn as I go. As one gets more mature, the run-of-the-mill problems become easier to handle. They don't loom as important."
....$50-$80

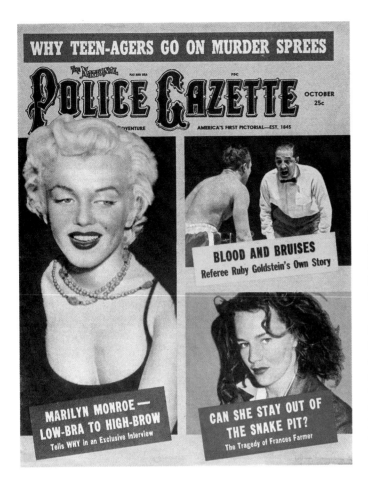

The National Police Gazette. October 1957. Unknown. This cover photo was taken in November 1954, the night that Marilyn met Ella Fitzgerald. Ella was Marilyn's favorite female singer. In the August 1972 issue of *MS* magazine, Ella had this to say about Marilyn: "I owe Marilyn Monroe a real debt. It was because of her that I played the Mocambo (an important Los Angeles club in the '50s). She personally called the owner of the Mocambo, and told him she wanted me booked immediately, and if he would do it, she would take a front table every night. She told him—and it was true, due to Marilyn's superstar status—that the press would go wild. The owner said yes, and Marilyn was there, front table, every night. The press went overboard...After that, I never had to play a small jazz club again. She was an unusual woman—a little ahead of her times. And she didn't know it." ....$20-$40

Hafta. 1955. Turkey. Unknown. This cover features a publicity photo for *The Seven Year Itch*, taken in 1955. That year, *Modern Screen* magazine reported that Marilyn always stopped for kids wanting her autograph. Marilyn always gave the public credit for her rise to fame and was especially fond of children. ....$40-$70

Visto. August 27, 1955. Italy. Unknown. Marilyn is seen here on the night of March 9, 1955, when she served as usherette at the premiere of *East of Eden* at the Astor Theatre in New York.
....$50-$90

Parts Pups. May 1955. Unknown. Marilyn is shown here riding a pink elephant at Madison Square Garden on March 30, 1955. The event was a benefit for the Arthritis and Rheumatism Foundation. It was Marilyn's idea to have the elephant painted pink.
....$60-$120

Marilyn Monroe – Her Last Untold Secrets. 1962. United States. Possibly Hal Berg. This is one of three magazines that came out in the U.S. shortly after Marilyn's death that were entirely about her. The cover photo was taken in 1955.
....$40-$80

SCOOP! VERY INTIMATE PICS OF BRANDO

MOVIE LIFE

MOVIE LIFE/**APRIL** 25c

PDC

HOLLYWOOD LOVE, SEX AND DATING

DEBRA PAGET:
how far should a girl go?

TAB HUNTER:
I stopped looking for love

TONY & JANET:
making kisses count

SHIRLEY JONES:
how to chase wolves

MARILYN MONROE

Movie Life. April 1956. United States. Possibly Hal Berg. This cover photo was taken in 1955. When reporters asked Marilyn about her bedroom voice, she replied, "I never talk in the bedroom."

....$65-$100

Modern Screen. June 1955. United States. Hal Berg. This cover photo was taken in New York in 1955. This issue reports that Marilyn had recently attended a birthday party at Toots Shor's in New York, and she got splinters when she sat down in a wooden chair! It also says that she threw a surprise party for Milton Berle at his studio. ....$40-$65

Screen Stories. July 1957. United States. Possibly Hal Berg. This cover photo was taken in 1955. Joshua Logan, who directed Marilyn in *Bus Stop*, once called her "one of the most unappreciated people in the world." ....$40-$60

Garbo. September 17, 1955. Spain. Unknown.
Though recently divorced, Marilyn's former husband,
Joe DiMaggio, accompanied her to the premiere of
The Seven Year Itch at Loew's State Theatre in New York
on June 1, 1955, which happened to be Marilyn's
29th birthday. It was the first and only time that
Joe escorted Marilyn to a major event.
....$40-$60

Noir Et Blanc. December 6, 1967. France. Unknown.
This cover features a photo of Marilyn in New York in
December 1955 at the premiere of *Rose Tattoo*.
When asked by a reporter if she would ever quit making
movies, Marilyn replied: "Only if I have to. And by that
I mean only if the public stops accepting me. I've worked
too hard to get where I am. Besides, it's part of me now.
It would be like cutting something vital out of me."
....$60-$90

The National Police Gazette. January 1959. United States. Unknown.
This photo was taken after a strap on Marilyn's dress had broken during a
press conference with Laurence Olivier on February 9, 1956. The two had
paired up to announce the planned production of Terrance Rattigan's play,
The Sleeping Prince. The event took place in the Terrace Room of the
Plaza Hotel in New York City. During a 1959 interview, Marilyn made the
following comment to reporter Lou Gerard, "A broken shoulder strap is a
heck of a lot sexier—or can be in the right hands—than a gown cut way
down to here." ("Here" was in the general vicinity of the navel.)
....$40-$60

Se Og Hor. October 5, 1956. Denmark. Cecil Beaton. This cover photo was taken in 1956. Cecil Beaton once said of Marilyn: "If this star is an abandoned sprite, she touchingly looks to her audience for approval. She is strikingly like an overexcited child asked downstairs after tea."

....$40-$70

Billed Bladet. February 12, 1957. Denmark. Cecil Beaton. This cover photo was taken in 1956. Cecil Beaton once said, "Miss Marilyn Monroe calls to mind the bouquet of a fireworks display."
....$60-$100

Kristall. 1961. Germany. Milton H. Greene. This cover depicts a photo of Marilyn from the famous black fishnet series of photos taken by Greene in 1956. During an interview in 1959, reporter Lou Gerard asked Marilyn if she ever felt revulsion towards the millions of lip-smacking wolves. She replied: "How can you feel like that about the most normal and natural reaction in the world? Anyway, a woman projecting from a screen, she's just an image. I'm personal, you know."
....$75-$100

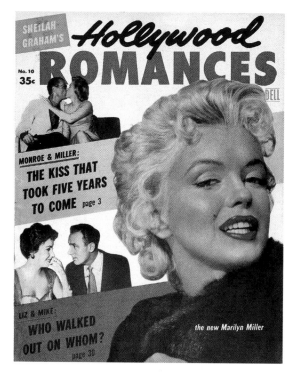

Cine Revue. July 20, 1956. France. Milton H. Greene. Marilyn poses here in front of her home at 595 Beverly Glen Boulevard, West Los Angeles, California, in 1956.
....$50-$80

Hollywood Romances. 1956. United States. Milton H. Greene. This cover features a 1956 publicity photo of Marilyn for *Bus Stop*. When quizzed about her chronic lateness, Marilyn once said: "It's not really me that's late. It's the others who are in such a hurry."
....$25-$45

Antena. May 13, 1958. Argentina. Milton H. Greene.
This cover features a publicity still of Marilyn for *Bus Stop*, taken in 1956. During an interview in 1959, reporter Lou Gerard asked Marilyn how the unified thinking of millions of men affected her. She replied: "Oh, I loved it, for two reasons. The first is obvious: Any woman loves that kind of tribute. The second is simple, too: When you can affect men like that, you're bound to become a star. I wanted to be a somebody more than anything in the world."
....$60-$90

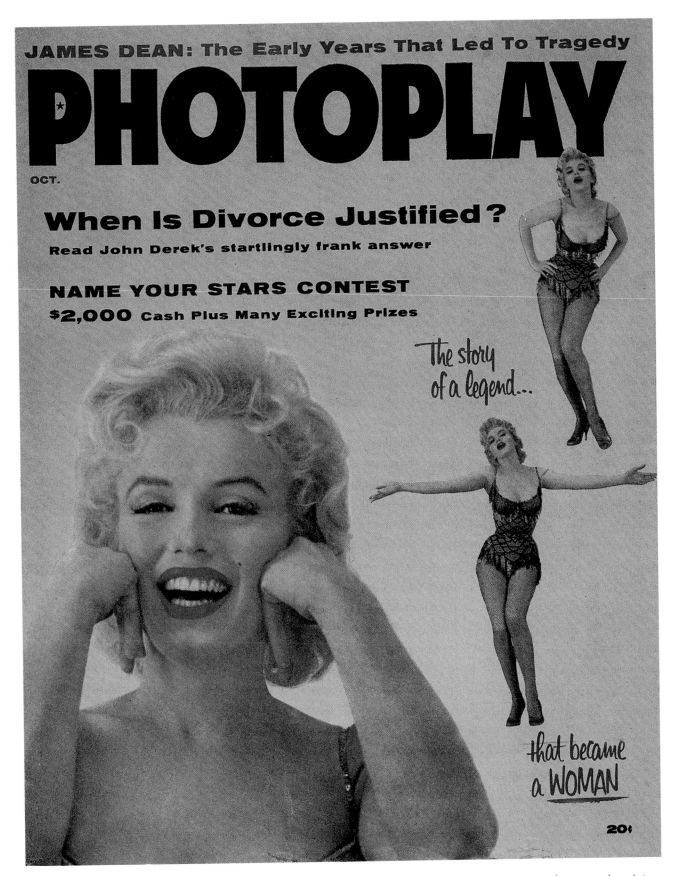

Photoplay. October 1956. United States. Frank Powolny. This cover features three publicity photos of Marilyn taken in May 1956 to promote her role in *Bus Stop*. Marilyn's third husband, Arthur Miller, once said: "I took her as a serious actress before I ever met her. I think she's an adroit comedienne, but I also think that she might turn into the greatest tragic actress that can be imagined." How prophetic these words are in retrospect. ....$50-$100

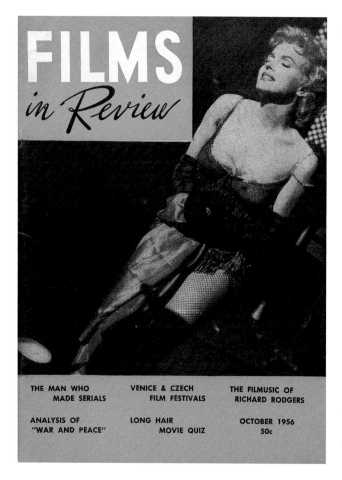

Films in Review. October 1956. United States. Milton H. Greene. This cover features Marilyn in a publicity still for *Bus Stop*, taken circa April 1956.
....$40-$60

Picture Show. October 13, 1956. England. Unknown. Marilyn embraces her co-star Don Murray in this 1956 scene still for *Bus Stop*. Reporters once asked Marilyn whether all her fans were male. She replied, "I haven't taken a sexus—I mean, a census."
....$30-$40

Hjemmet
NR. 5   29. JANUAR 1957   PRIS 85 ØRE

Filmene, vi venter på -

Den dyre og den billige husmoder – læs side 16

Hvem vandt hobby-konkurrencens 45 præmier? Se side 41

I dette nummer startes en serie filmromaner bygget over de blokerede amerikanske film. Den første er

BUS STOP
med Marilyn Monroe

Følg med fra begyndelsen

Hjemmet. January 29, 1957. Denmark. Unknown. This cover depicts Marilyn and her co-star Don Murray in a scene still for *Bus Stop*, taken in 1956. Poet Carl Sandburg once said of Marilyn: "She was not the usual movie idol. There was something democratic about her. She was the type who would join in and wash up the supper dishes even if you didn't ask her."

....$50-$80

Marilyn Monroe – The Complete Story of Her Life, Her Loves and Her Death. 1962. United States. Unknown. This cover features a publicity photo of Marilyn wearing a costume from *Bus Stop* and was taken in 1956. This issue was entirely devoted to Marilyn.

....$40-$80

MARILYN MONROE
THE COMPLETE STORY OF HER LIFE, HER LOVES AND HER DEATH
35c
ICD

ABC. July 7, 1956. Belgium. Unknown. Marilyn is seen here during a press conference in 1956, regarding her film, *Bus Stop*. The Russian magazine *Nedyela* once wrote: "When you speak of the American way of life, everybody thinks of chewing gum, Coca-Cola, and Marilyn Monroe."

....$60-$90

Sabado Grafico. August 11, 1962. Spain. Unknown. This cover photo was taken in June 1956 during an interview Marilyn gave to members of the press. She announced that she would wed playwright Arthur Miller. When one female reporter asked her how many children she planned to have, she coyly answered, "Why, I'm not married yet, dear." ....$50-$80

Paris Match. July 7, 1956. France. Paul Slade. Marilyn is shown here with her third husband, Arthur Miller. The photo was taken in 1956. After Marilyn's death, Arthur said of Marilyn, "She never had enough faith in herself." ....$40-$60

145

Billed Bladet. July 10, 1956. Denmark. Unknown. This cover photo was taken in 1956. Shortly after Marilyn's death, Arthur Miller proclaimed: "With a little luck, I think she could have made it…She never really had a chance." ....$40-$60

Idolos. July 17, 1958. Spain. Unknown. This cover features a candid photo of Marilyn, taken in England in 1956 while Marilyn was there to film *The Prince and the Showgirl*. The entire issue was about Marilyn.
 ....$50-$75

Sissi. August 24, 1959. Spain. Unknown. This cover photo features a photo of Marilyn and her third husband, Arthur Miller. The photo was taken in 1956. During her marriage to Miller, Marilyn proclaimed, "I don't think I'm a good wife yet, but I sure am trying, for I've found, now at last, this man who means the most to me." Arthur said, "She has made me feel like a new man at 41." ....$40-$50

Parade. January 27, 1957. United States. Lloyd Shearer. This cover photo was taken at London's Heathrow Airport in 1956, as Marilyn was arriving to begin shooting *The Prince and the Showgirl*. Photographer Elliot Erwitt once said this about Marilyn: "I had always thought that all those amusing remarks she was supposed to have made for the press had probably been manufactured and mimeographed by her press agent, but they weren't. She was a very bright person, an instinctive type." ....$40-$70

Meridiano. January 10, 1960. Italy. Unknown. This cover features a photo of Marilyn taken in London in 1956, on the day she arrived to begin filming *The Prince and the Showgirl*. Marilyn once said: "Fame doesn't have anything to do with my life. That's not where I live." ....$50-$80

147

MARILINA E IL FUTURO PAPÀ

«Il principe dormiente» è il titolo del nuovo film che Marilyn Monroe e Laurence Olivier, qui fotografati al Savoy Hotel di Londra, hanno incominciato in questi giorni a girare insieme. Vivien Leigh, la moglie di Laurence, ha annunciato, nel frattempo, di aspettare un bambino, dopo 17 anni di matrimonio.

SPEDIZ. IN ABBONAM. POSTALE - GRUPPO II MILANO

NOVELLA
Esce il giovedì

ANNO XXXVII - N. 32
5 AGOSTO 1956
LIRE 50

Novella. August 5, 1956. Italy. Unknown. Marilyn is seen here with Sir Laurence Olivier at a press conference on July 15, 1956, announcing the pair's upcoming film, *The Prince and the Showgirl*. Upon Marilyn's arrival in London in July 1956 to shoot the film, *The London Evening News* proclaimed: "She walks. She talks. She really is as luscious as strawberries and cream."

....$50-$75

Fotogramas. July 27, 1956. Spain. Unknown. This cover depicts Marilyn Monroe and Laurence Olivier during a press conference held at the Savoy Hotel in London, England on July 16, 1956. The two were announcing that they would soon begin filming of *The Sleeping Prince* (later renamed *The Prince and the Showgirl*).
....$50-$75

Picture Show. July 4, 1957. England. Milton H. Greene. This cover photo, taken in 1956, depicts Marilyn Monroe and Sir Laurence Olivier in a scene still from *The Prince and the Showgirl*. Marilyn once commented: "Johnny Hyde was wonderful, but he was not my Svengali. Milton Greene was not my Svengali…I'm nobody's slave and never have been…Now they write that Lee Strasberg is my Svengali… and Arthur Miller isn't my Svengali."
....$30-$50

Mon Film. December 4, 1957. France. Milton H. Greene. This cover photo was taken in 1956 and depicts Marilyn in a costume worn in the 1957 film, *The Prince and the Showgirl*. Marilyn once lamented, "Why haven't I the right to grow and expand like everybody else?"
....$30-$50

Weekend. April 9, 1960. Australia. Unknown.
The cover of this magazine features a rare candid photo
of Marilyn and her third husband, Arthur Miller, while in
London in August 1956 to film *The Prince and the Showgirl*.
....$60-$90

Oggi. September 25, 1958. Italy. Jack Cardiff.
Cardiff was the preferred photographer of Britain's royal
family. He took this cover photo of Marilyn in 1956. During
an interview, Marilyn once commented, "Gee,
happiness wasn't anything I ever took for granted."
....$40-$65

OGGI

ANNO XII - N. 45 - 8 NOVEMBRE 1956 • SETTIMANALE DI POLITICA ATTUALITÀ E CULTURA • SPED. ABB. POST. GR. II - LIRE SESSANTA

LA REGINA DELLA CELLULOIDE

E LA REGINA D'INGHILTERRA

SI STRINGONO LA MANO

Oggi. November 8, 1956. Italy. Unknown.
Marilyn is seen here as she meets Queen Elizabeth while in England to shoot *The Prince and the Showgirl*. Marilyn was requested to appear at a Royal Command Film Performance at the Empire Theatre in London on October 29, 1956.
....$40-$60

Star Revue. May 1960. Germany. Richard Avedon.
This cover photo was taken in 1957. Marilyn once commented: "I'm a failure as a woman. My men expect so much of me because of the image they've made of me, and that I've made of myself, as a sex symbol. Men expect so much, and I can't live up to it. They expect bells to ring and whistles to whistle, but my anatomy is the same as any other woman's. I can't live up to it."
....$60-$90

STAR REVUE

Spätheimkehrerin Marlene Dietrich
Mr. Bardot kann B.B. nicht vergessen
Hilde Knef: Die Presse hat schuld

NR. 10 / MAI 1960 - 13. JAHRG. · POSTKENNZEICHEN: C 6652 D · 70 PF.

FERNSEHEN · FILM · SCHALLPLATTE

Giesler-Mandantin:
MARILYN MONROE

New York Mirror Magazine. June 22, 1957. United States. Richard Avedon. This cover photo was taken in 1957. Marilyn was photographed in this gown for publicity photos promoting *The Prince and the Showgirl*. She wore the gown to the *April in Paris* ball at the Waldorf Astoria in New York in 1957, accompanied by her third husband, Arthur Miller . Actor Laurence Olivier once made the following remark about Marilyn: "Look at that face. She could be five years old."

....$100-$200

Tempo. August 27, 1960. Italy. Richard Avedon. This cover photo was taken in 1957. Marilyn once said: "The most unsatisfactory men are those who pride themselves on their virility and regard sex as if it were some form of athletics at which you win cups. It is a woman's spirit and mood a man has to stimulate in order to make sex interesting. The real lover is the man who can thrill you just by touching your head or smiling into your eyes or by just staring into space."
....$50-$80

Neue Illustrierte. October 22, 1960. Germany. Richard Avedon. This photo of Marilyn was taken in 1957. Marilyn once commented to a reporter: "I am beginning to have a clearer picture of who I am. I like some of it and dislike some of it. All these opinions from outsiders are just too general. I don't think they have substance."
....$60-$80

Cinema. 1957. Lisbon. Unknown.
Marilyn and Laurence Olivier embrace in this 1957 publicity photo for *The Prince and the Showgirl*. This photo was used on many of the movie posters for the film. After filming completed, Marilyn made the following statement to the cast and crew: "I hope you will all forgive me. It wasn't my fault. I've been sick all through the picture. Please, please, don't hold it against me."
....$50-$85

Pix. January 10, 1959. Australia. Unknown. This cover features a 1958 publicity still for *Some Like It Hot*, which was released in 1959. Marilyn reluctantly took the role of Sugar Kane in the film, only because of mounting bills she and Arthur Miller had incurred.
....$60-$100

Detective Cronaca. July 30, 1960. Italy. Unknown. Marilyn is seen here in a 1958 scene still from her role as Sugar Kane in the 1959 film, *Some Like It Hot*. Marilyn once said: "I think that sexuality is only attractive when it's natural and spontaneous. Art comes from that—real art, everything."
....$40-$80

Parade. December 7, 1958 United States. Lloyd Shearer. This candid photo of Marilyn was taken on location during the filming of *Some Like It Hot* in 1958. Shooting took place both inside and outside of the famous Hotel Del Coronado in San Diego, California.
....$60-$90

Pix. April 11, 1959. Australia. Unknown. This cover features a 1958 publicity still for *Some Like It Hot*. Marilyn was pregnant during filming and later suffered a miscarriage. She once said, "Someday I want to have children and give them all the love I never had."
....$60-$100

March 1959 • 35c

COSMOPOLITAN

SPECIAL ISSUE ## Manners and Morals

Swap-Mate Scandals ▪ He-Men and Honor in Business
Our Moral Revolt from 1920 to 1960 ▪ Is Divorce a Disease?
Lovelorn Sob Sisters ▪ Parents Review Sex Education

The New Marilyn
"SOME LIKE IT HOT"

Listening Walls — Margaret Millar's Great New Mystery Novel

Cosmopolitan. March 1959. United States. Artwork by Jon Whitcomb. Marilyn is depicted here in a costume worn in *Some Like It Hot*. Marilyn walked off the set during filming in 1958, and proclaimed: "I'm not going back into that film until Wilder reshoots my opening. When Marilyn Monroe comes into a room, nobody's going to be looking at Tony Curtis playing Joan Crawford. They're going to be looking at Marilyn Monroe."

..........$50-$100

New Screen News. October 2, 1959. Australia. Unknown. This cover features a 1958 publicity still for *Some Like It Hot*. The film was recently voted the greatest comedic film of all time. Marilyn once commented: "...But sex is not enough. My public is growing up just as I am. After all, I'm not 19 anymore and if I stick with the sex bit, who will be paying to see me when I'm 50?"
....$40-$60

Showcase. Australia. February 1961. Richard Avedon. Marilyn is shown on this cover in a publicity still taken in November 1958 for *Some Like It Hot*. The whole series of photos from this session had to be heavily touched up, as Marilyn had gained so much weight prior to filming, due to her pregnancy. The photos were blown up to 8" x 10", and the extra weight was simply "trimmed" off of Marilyn before their release.
....$40-$70

Marie Claire. September 1959. France. Richard Avedon. This cover features a publicity photo of Marilyn taken in 1959. Marilyn once commented: "A woman can't be alone. She needs a man. A man and a woman support and strengthen each other. She just can't do it by herself."
....$60-$80

NR. 34. OFFENBURG, 22. AUG. 1962. 3 Z 2013 C. 60 PFENNIG

BUNTE
ILLUSTRIERTE

Münchner
ILLUSTRIERTE

Neuer
Fortsetzungsbericht
Marilyn Monroe
EIN LEBEN OHNE HAPPY END

10 Seiten
Farbbericht:
DIE DONAU

Bunte Illustrierte. August 22, 1962. Germany. Richard Avedon. Marilyn graces this cover in a publicity photo taken in 1959. Marilyn once said: "I think I have one talent. I think it's observing. I hope that it adds up to acting. I hope to put it to good use."

....$60-$85

158

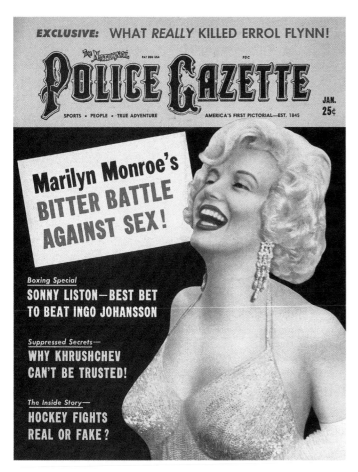

EXCLUSIVE: WHAT *REALLY* KILLED ERROL FLYNN!

The National POLICE GAZETTE

PAT SEO USA   PDC

JAN. 25¢

SPORTS • PEOPLE • TRUE ADVENTURE   AMERICA'S FIRST PICTORIAL—EST. 1845

Marilyn Monroe's BITTER BATTLE AGAINST SEX!

Boxing Special
SONNY LISTON—BEST BET TO BEAT INGO JOHANSSON

Suppressed Secrets—
WHY KHRUSHCHEV CAN'T BE TRUSTED!

The Inside Story—
HOCKEY FIGHTS REAL OR FAKE ?

The National Police Gazette. January 1960. United States. Unknown. Marilyn is shown here at the premiere of *Some Like It Hot* at Loew's Capitol Theater in New York on March 29, 1959. She once described the event: "This was at the opening in New York of *Some Like It Hot*…Smile, they said, and I obliged. My husband (Arthur Miller) waited patiently. Mr. Kenneth, of Lilly Dache, did my hair, and John Moore did my dress—just soufflé, with beads, nothing else. Oh, yes, and the earrings designed especially— long rhinestones that would keep moving." On March 8, 1960, she won a Golden Globe Award for "Best Actress in a Comedy" for her performance in the film.
....$40-$60

VISTO Marilyn Monroe intervistata dice: "Mio marito è noioso"

ANNO IX - N. 41 - MILANO 6 OTTOBRE 1960   LIRE 80

Come sarà l'uomo nel prossimo futuro
SI PREPARA LA MACCHINA DELLA VITA
Una madre-artificiale per salvare i nati prematuri
★
Gli assurdi d'oggi
L'assassino circola fra la gente
E può uccidere ancora

FORSE FINISCE ANCHE L'AMORE DI MARILYN

Visto. October 6, 1960. Italy. Unknown. Marilyn is seen her as she arrives at the Italian Consulate in New York to receive the David Di Donatello Prize (the Italian Oscar) in 1959. She won the award for "Best Foreign Actress of 1958," based on her performance in the *Prince and the Showgirl*.
....$60-$80

DIVAGANDO 30¢

THE LEADING ITALIAN WEEKLY MAGAZINE IN THE U.S.   30 MAGGIO 1959   VOL. XXXIII - N. 621

Divagando. May 30, 1959. United States. Unknown. The cover photo on this magazine was taken at the Italian Consulate in New York in 1959, as Marilyn accepted the aforementioned David Di Donatello Prize. Marilyn once said: "My work is the only ground I've ever had to stand on. To put it bluntly, I seem to have a whole superstructure with no foundation, but I'm working on the foundation."
....$70-$125

159

Bravo. July 17-23, 1960. Germany. Unknown.
This cover features a publicity still used to promote
Let's Make Love, released in 1960. Marilyn once said,
"Dogs never bite me—just humans."
....$40-$60

Stage and Cinema. April 1, 1960. South Africa. Unknown.
This cover features a publicity still taken in 1959 to promote
Marilyn's 1960 film, *Let's Make Love*. Marilyn once
commented: "I don't consider myself an intellectual. And this
is not one of my aims. But I admire intellectual people."
....$100-$120

intervalo de cine. 1963. Argentina. Unknown.
This South American cover features a publicity still taken in 1959 to promote *Let's Make Love*. Marilyn once commented: "I used to get the feeling, and sometimes I still get it, that I was fooling somebody— I don't know who or what—maybe myself. I have feelings some days when there are scenes with a lot of responsibility, and I'll wish, 'Gee, if only I would have been a cleaning woman.' "
....$40-$70

Gaceta Illustrada. August 11, 1962. Spain. Unknown.
A rather stressed Marilyn is seen here in a photo taken in 1959, prior to filming *Let's Make Love*. After Marilyn was fired during the filming of *Something's Got to Give* in 1962, she commented: "An actor is supposed to be a sensitive instrument. Isaac Stern takes good care of his violin. What if everybody jumped on his violin?…It seems to me it's time they stopped knocking their assets around."
....$60-$90

TV and Movie Screen. September 1960. United States. Unknown.
This cover photo was taken in January 1960 during a reception that was thrown for Yves Montand, Marilyn's co-star in *Let's Make Love*. Marilyn once proclaimed: "I'm looking forward to becoming a marvelous—excuse the word *marvelous*—character actress. Like Marie Dressler, like Will Rogers."
....$35-$50

161

Funk und Film. December 10, 1960. Germany. Unknown.
This cover features a 1960 publicity photo for *Let's Make Love*.
During filming, Marilyn made the following notation in her notebook:
"What am I afraid of? Do I think I can't act? I know I can act, but I
am afraid. I am afraid, and I should not be and I must not be."
....$50-$70

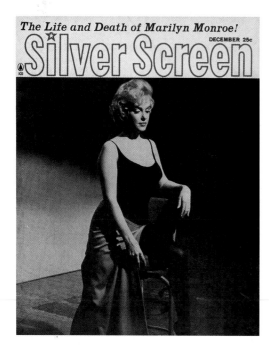

Silver Screen. December 1962. United States. Unknown.
This photo of a sad-looking Marilyn was taken in January 1960 during
the filming of *Let's Make Love*. Marilyn once said: "I'm tired of
playing sex kittens…I want roles that I can get my teeth into, roles
that enable me to show a side of myself which appeals to an intelligent
public."
....$20-$40

Everybody's. September 19, 1962. Australia. Unknown.
This cover features a film still of Marilyn taken in the spring of 1960 to
promote *Let's Make Love*. In 1961, Marilyn proclaimed: "As of today,
I have absolutely no regrets. I think I am a mature person now who
can take things in stride. I'm grateful for people in my past. They
helped me get to where I am, wherever that is. But now, I'm thinking
for myself and sitting in on all business transactions."
....$60-$90

OGGI

ANNO XVIII · NUMERO 33 - 16 AGOSTO 1962 ★ SETTIMANALE DI POLITICA ATTUALITÀ E CULTURA ★ SPED. ABB. POST. GR. II · LIRE OTTANTA

MARILYN AVEVA GIÀ TENTATO DI UCCIDERSI: OGGI POSSO RACCONTARE COME LA SALVAI

Da questo numero:

PARLA LA PIÙ INTIMA AMICA DELLA DIVA

DIETRO IL SUO SORRISO ERA NASCOSTA DA TEMPO UNA PROFONDA TRAGEDIA

Marilyn Monroe, una donna che dalla vita sembrava avere avuto tutto: la bellezza, la fama, la ricchezza, l'amore. Eppure pochi sapevano che dietro a quel sorriso di bambola si nascondeva un'insoddisfazione profonda, un senso tragico del vuoto. La donna tanto invidiata era in realtà una creatura sola e infelice. È questa solitudine, forse, che ha indotto Marilyn a compiere il gesto disperato che l'ha uccisa: inghiottire, il 4 agosto, un tubetto di sonnifero. Già una volta ella aveva tentato di togliersi la vita ed era stata salvata all'ultimo momento dalla sua amica intima Natacha Lytess: è la stessa Natacha che racconta ora questo episodio nel primo articolo di un'eccezionale serie che cominciamo a pubblicare da questo numero alle pagine 16-25. Si tratta di un ritratto inedito della grande scomparsa: un documento umano e giornalistico di altissimo interesse.

Oggi. August 16, 1962. Italy. Unknown. This photo of Marilyn was taken in 1960 to promote her newest film, *Let's Make Love*. Marilyn once said: "Some of those bastards in Hollywood wanted me to drop Arthur. Said it would ruin my career. They're born cowards and want you to be like them. One reason I want to see Kennedy win is that Nixon's associated with that whole scene." ....$50-$80

This Week Magazine. August 20, 1960. United States. Don Ornitz. Marilyn and co-star Yves Montand are seen here in a publicity still for *Let's Make Love*. Marilyn once commented: "I think that when you are famous, every weakness is exaggerated."
....$40-$60

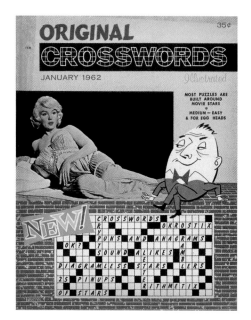

Original Crosswords. January 1962. United States. Unknown. This unusual cover on a crossword magazine feature's a 1960 publicity still of Marilyn from *Let's Make Love*. Marilyn once commented: "I don't know if high society is different in other cities, but in Hollywood, important people can't stand to be invited someplace that isn't full of other important people. They don't mind a few unfamous people being present because they make good listeners. But if a star or studio chief or any other great movie personages find themselves sitting among a lot of nobodies, they get frightened—as if somebody was trying to demote them."
....$25-$55

Piccolo. November 6, 1960. Holland. Unknown. This photo of a melancholy Marilyn was taken on the set of *Let's Make Love* in 1960. Marilyn once said: "I once wanted to prove myself by being a great actress. Now I want to prove I'm a person. Then maybe I'll be a great actress."
....$50-$75

stern. September 17, 1960. Germany. John Bryson.
This photo shows Marilyn and co-star Yves Montand in a publicity still
for *Let's Make Love*. Marilyn once commented, "Next to my husband,
and along with Marlon Brando, I think that Yves Montand is the most
attractive man I've ever met."
....$50-$80

Successo. September 1960. Italy. Jerome Zerbe. Marilyn is seen here
with her co-star Yves Montand from *Let's Make Love*. The pair had
an affair both on-screen and off. Marilyn once said: "I like actors
very much, but to marry one would be like marrying your brother.
You look too much alike in the mirror."
....$50-$90

Tempo. April 11, 1961. Denmark. Unknown.
Three film greats—Marilyn Monroe, Clark Gable, and
Montgomery Clift—pose for this 1960 publicity photo
for *The Misfits*. It would be the last film that
Marilyn and Clark would complete
before their deaths.
....$60-$90

Weekend. March 1-5, 1961. England. Unknown. Marilyn is seen here relaxing between scenes on the set of her 1961 film, *The Misfits*. Filming began the third week of July1960 near Reno, Nevada, with temperatures soaring to 110 degrees. Marilyn had to be hospitalized during filming for a variety of problems, and this cover photo of her was taken in September, after her return from the hospital. Shortly after filming, Marilyn commented to a reporter: "I am trying to find myself as a person. Sometimes that's not easy."
....$60-$90

Cinelandia. June 1961. Brazil. Unknown. This cover features a photo of Marilyn taken in August 1960 during filming of *The Misfits*. Marilyn once said: "I don't look at myself as a commodity, but I'm sure a lot of people have. Including, well, one corporation in particular, which shall be nameless."
....$50-$70

ABC. April 15, 1961. Holland. Unknown. Marilyn Monroe and Clark Gable stare into each other's eyes in this publicity still for *The Misfits*, taken in 1960. Gable died of a heart attack just weeks after filming was completed.
....$35-$65

Mañana Julio 1 de 1961 No. 931 Precio $2.50

ANALISIS POLITICO
BERLIN
PAZ O
GUERRA
ATOMICA

MARILYN MONROE

Mañana. July 1, 1961. Mexico. Unknown. This pensive photo of Marilyn was taken on the set of *The Misfits* in 1960. Marilyn once said: "I think that we're rushing too much these days. That's why people get nervous. I feel that I'm not in this big American rush."

....$100-$150

167

Piccolo. September 2 1962. Holland. Probably Eve Arnold. Marilyn is seen here in a publicity still taken in 1960 for her 1961 film, *The Misfits*, which co-starred Clark Gable, Montgomery Clift, and Eli Wallach. Marilyn's marriage with Arthur Miller was crumbling during filming. After their divorce, and shortly before her death, Marilyn commented: "With everything, I'm still, I suppose, alone. In a way, I'm freer than I've ever been...I enjoy knowing that I'm alive. And you can underline 'alive.' It's better to be unhappy alone than unhappy with someone."
....$50-$80

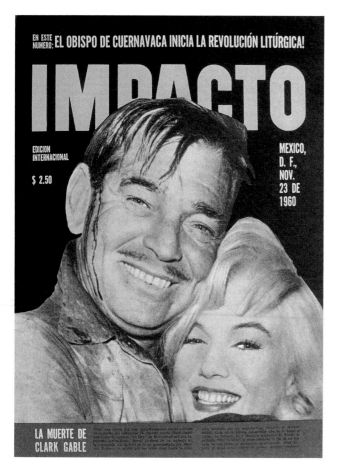

Impacto. November 23, 1960. Mexico. Unknown. Marilyn and her idol, Clark Gable, embrace in this publicity still for *The Misfits*, taken in 1960. During an interview, Marilyn remarked: "Well, I know I've been invited places to sort of, you know, brighten up a dinner table. It's sort of like being a musician; you're invited so you can play."
....$75-$100

JOURS DE FRANCE

le drame de MARILYN

N° 327 - 1 NF
18 FÉVRIER 1961

Jours De France. February 18, 1961. France. Eve Arnold. This stunning close-up of Marilyn was taken about the time she was filming *The Misfits* in 1960. When a reporter asked Marilyn, "How do you account for three marriages going up the creek?", she replied, "No lifeguards around that little old creek."

....$60-$90

Woman's Day. March 19, 1962. Australia. Unknown. This cover photo of Marilyn was taken in 1961. Very few photos of Marilyn taken in 1961 were used on magazine covers.
....$40-$80

Magazine De Novedades. March 4, 1962. Mexico. Unknown. This photo of Marilyn was taken in February 1962 while she was in Mexico shopping for furniture to furnish her new home in Brentwood, California. This photo was taken at a press conference held at the Continental Hilton Hotel in Mexico City. Marilyn was later buried in the same pale sea-green Pucci dress she wore for this conference.
....$60-$100

Magazine De Novedades. August 12, 1962. Mexico. Unknown. Marilyn had just been in Mexico on a shopping trip in February 1962 and made the cover of this magazine at the same time. Just five months later, the magazine once again featured her on the cover, announcing her untimely death at age 36. After Marilyn's death, Hollywood columnist Hedda Hopper stated: "In a way, we are all guilty. We built her to the skies. We loved her, but left her lonely and afraid when she needed us most."
....$60-$100

ecran. August 24, 1962. Chile. Unknown. This candid photo of Marilyn was taken while she was in Mexico City in February 1962 on a shopping trip. Marilyn once commented: "I remember the day when I was a kid that Will Rogers died in a plane crash. It was very meaningful to me. Or when my idol Jean Harlow died. I never forgot it. It was so tragic. I cried for days when I thought about it. Yet now I wonder. It might be kind of a relief to be finished."
....$30-$40

L'Europeo. March 25, 1962. Italy. Unknown. Marilyn is shown here at the Golden Globe Awards in March 1962. She was voted "World Film Favorite" of 1961. Rock Hudson presented the award. Marilyn attended the event with her boyfriend Jose Bolanos, a Mexican film writer/producer that she had met on her trip to Mexico to buy furniture for her new Brentwood home.
....$40-$60

Films in Review. June-July 1963. United States. Unknown. Marilyn is seen here in a still from her last (uncompleted) film, *Something's Got to Give*, 1962. Marilyn once said: "I guess I knew it all the time. I knew I belonged to the public and to the world. The public was the only family, the only Prince Charming, and the only home I had ever dreamed about."
....$15-$35

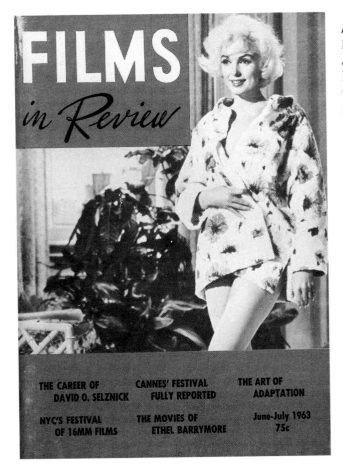

SETTIMANA ILLUSTRATA

INCOM

ANNO XV - N. 23 - 10 GIUGNO 1962 ★ POLITICA · ATTUALITÀ · CULTURA ★ SPEDIZIONE IN ABBONAMENTO POST. · GRUPPO II ★ LIRE OTTANTA

Nell'interno

LE SCONVOLGENTI IMMAGINI DEL DISASTRO DI VOGHERA

L'AMERICA È SCANDALIZZATA

DALLA DECISIONE DI MARILYN

DI POSARE NUDA IN UN FILM

Una espressione assorta di Marilyn Monroe, l'attrice che ha mobilitato tutte le leghe americane della decenza a causa della sua decisione di posare completamente svestita in una scena del suo nuovo film « Qualcosa da offrire ». All'inizio della sua carriera, Marilyn posò nuda come modella fotografica per un calendario e quella foto le viene rinfacciata ancora oggi dalle associazioni moralistiche degli Stati Uniti. La decisione di Marilyn di ripetere quell'esibizione ha scandalizzato l'opinione pubblica, ma l'attrice ha dichiarato di esserne stupita. « Penso », ha detto, « che sia una scena castigatissima, nonostante ci si aspetti il contrario ». Secondo gli amici di Marilyn la decisione dell'attrice è legata al timore, per lei divenuto ossessionante, di invecchiare. Marilyn ha paura che il pubblico l'abbandoni, teme di rimanere sola e dimenticata. Ed è soprattutto per convincere se stessa che questo pericolo è ancora lontano che accetta di esibirsi in una scena audace. « Finché si parlerà di me, in bene o in male », ha detto, « sarò ancora giovane e viva ». Ora l'attrice si è legata sentimentalmente a un giovane messicano. Nell'interno, alle pagine 50, 51, 52 e 53, un grande servizio fotografico sulla scena del bagno interpretata da Marilyn.

Settimana Incom Illustrada. June 10, 1962. Italy. Unknown. This candid photo of Marilyn was taken during filming of *Something's Got to Give* in April 1962, just a few months before she died. The last words Marilyn spoke on the movie screen were in *The Misfits*: "How do you find your way back in the dark?"

....$40-$70

Index

About the Author

Clark Kidder resides in rural Wisconsin, where he and his wife, Linda, and their two sons, Robby and Nathan, farm 200 acres of land.

Drawing from his expertise, Kidder has authored several books on Marilyn Monroe, including: *Marilyn Monroe UnCovers* (Quon Editions, 1994), *Marilyn Monroe Collectibles* (HarperCollins, 1999), *Marilyn Monroe—Cover to Cover* (Krause Publications, 1999), and *Marilyn Memorabilia* (Krause Publications, 2002). Kidder is also the author of *Orphan Trains and Their Precious Cargo* (Heritage Books, Inc., 2001) and director of the Wisconsin Orphan Train Research Center. He further writes freelance articles for magazines around the world. He is also president of the newly formed *Kidder Productions*.

As a specialist in appraising Marilyn Monroe items, Kidder receives calls, letters, and faxes daily from collectors around the world, wanting to purchase, trade, and sell Marilyn memorabilia—or simply query the value of such items. He is constantly amazed at the number of new and previously unknown items that surface.

Kidder also happens to be his family's genealogist, having traced his Kidder roots back to 1320 in Maresfield, Sussex, England.